THE POTTERY AND PORCELAIN COLLECTOR'S HANDBOOK

A Guide *to* Early American Ceramics *from* Maine *to* California *by* William C. Ketchum, Jr.

Funk & Wagnalls   *New York*

Also by William C. Ketchum, Jr.

Early Potters and Potteries of New York State

To Rachael

CONTENTS

c. 1

Contents

II

STONEWARE

Techniques of Manufacture 49

III
BROWNWARE AND
YELLOW WARE

IV
WHITEWARES

Contents

PREFACE

For many reasons—sociologists have advanced a variety of explanatory theories ranging from natural acquisitiveness to an attempted partial withdrawal from today's complex and threatening world—the collecting of antique objects has become a veritable American mania. Furniture, silver, bottles, toys, clothing, and even barbed wire are eagerly sought, researched, and displayed by myriad persons across the face of the nation. Ceramics were among the first examples of domestic craftsmanship to be acquired by collectors, and the interest continues unabated.

As early as the 1890s antique enthusiasts were attracted to certain types of American pottery, particularly Pennsylvania and New England tablewares. At this time the first books on the subject were written, and since then numerous collectors' guides and ceramic histories have been published. Most of these have two common characteristics: an assumption, implicit in text and illustration, that the average antique collector is a wealthy man capable of purchasing what he desires regardless of cost, and a further conclusion that nearly all pottery worthy of notice was made in Ohio and the Northeast. The latter proposition was never valid. Beautiful and unusual pottery was made by artisans in all areas of the nation from Florida to Oregon. Moreover, the concept of the collector as millionaire if it was ever accurate, is no longer so. Particularly since the Second World War a veritable army of new antiquers has entered the field. Most of these are people of modest means who cannot afford to bid for the few pieces of Philadelphia porcelain or eighteenth-century stoneware that are not already in museum collections.

These new collectors are turning to fields, such as yellow ware and American ironstone, that were largely ignored by previous generations. They also show far more interest in learning the history of their local potters and potteries than in exploring the background of foreign artisans or those national figures whose work they are never likely to see outside a glass case. It is hoped that this book will provide such enthusiasts with a general guide to the varieties of old ceramics available to them and with a foundation upon which may be built a detailed knowledge of the craftsmen whose work they acquire.

In light of these goals the illustrations herein are designed to cover the common ceramic types most likely to be encountered in antique shops throughout the nation rather than the scarce museum pieces few of us can ever hope to own. Likewise, the text for the most part focuses not on such famous early potteries as Bennington and Boston, which have already been amply explored, but on obscure manufactories in states such as Arkansas, California, and Utah, kilns which, while today largely unknown, may be expected to assume a greater importance in future evaluations of the field.

Since most of the illustrations and some of the textual material is from local sources, I have often relied substantially upon ceramics authorities in the various states. I am grateful for their assistance and would especially like to express my appreciation to the following: Patrick Dunnahoe of Benton, Arkansas; Margaret Key of Santa Ana, California; William H. Bullard of Gainesville, Florida; Elfriede F. Rowe of Lawrence, Kansas; Betty I. Madden of Springfield, Illinois; Eugenia C. Holland of Baltimore, Maryland; Michael Brook of St. Paul, Minnesota; Roy M. Stubbs of Warrensburg, Missouri; Brad L. Rauschenberg of Winston-Salem, North Carolina; Arthur C. Spencer of Portland, Oregon; Harriett C. Meloy of Helena, Montana; Robert C. Pettit of Lincoln, Nebraska; Georgeanna H. Greer of San Antonio, Texas; Emma N. Mortensen of Hyrum, Utah; Robert G. Carroon of Milwaukee and Joan Severa of Madison, Wisconsin.

INTRODUCTION

The five general categories of American ceramics—redware, stoneware, yellow ware, whiteware, and porcelain—have provided collectors with a variety of interesting antiques for many years. This pottery and china, much of it handmade, falls readily into the category of folk art, either through shape and design or, as in the case of slip- or scratch-decorated pieces, through the illustrative motifs (birds, flowers, and the like) sketched on the clay surface.

One is immediately drawn to these simple, homey forms whose antecedents lie in a European ceramic tradition extending back over hundreds of years. Since our early provincial artisans were constantly being joined by others of their craft migrating from the continental potting centers, it is understandable that American pottery can never be viewed in isolation. It was always and is still today subject to the influence of foreign craftsmen. German stoneware techniques are reflected in mid-nineteenth-century Ohio salt-glazed pottery. Spanish, Dutch, and middle European slip-glazed decoration may often appear indistinguishable from Connecticut or Pennsylvania finishes. As various decorative styles swept over Europe, they were borne to these shores as well and, particularly after 1820, played a substantial role in altering our concepts of ceramic form and decoration. This was most noticeably the case in urban pottery centers such as Trenton, Philadelphia, and East Liverpool, where molding and other factory techniques encouraged mass production of ware consciously designed to imitate popular European types.

However, alongside this cosmopolitan industry there always existed an unchanging functional style, exemplified in household ceramics—red- and stoneware pots, jugs and tableware—which varied little from the seventeenth to the twentieth century. These plain forms, admirably suited to their respective purposes and often subtly decorated, are now considered by discerning collectors as being in the true American tradition, the product and reflection of our agrarian, westward-aspiring society of the last two centuries.

While the factory-made ware was largely confined to a few major Eastern, Atlantic Coast, and Midwestern centers, classic utilitarian pottery was turned out by craftsmen in tiny shops from Maine to Florida, and on through the mountain states to the Pacific Northwest. The South, in particular, may prove to be a veritable treasure house of nineteenth-century utilitarian ceramics. The field has scarcely been tapped.

The collector who will pursue these undiscovered and elusive objects with most success is the one whose knowledge of our domestic ceramics in general and his own area's products in particular is most acute. It is for this reason that I have attempted to set forth in this book at least some discussion of potters in every area of the country. However, because in many states research on the early ceramics industry is just beginning, and the collector who would obtain this information must often uncover it himself, it is important to learn the techniques and develop the skills required in such research.

Your first American ironstone platter or Rockingham doorstop usually comes as a surprise: a gift or, perhaps, an unexpected find in Grandmother's cellar. If the new piece isn't promptly relegated to the attic or pitched into the trash bin, the consequences are fairly predictable. Antiques are magnets; they attract like objects. In a short time one is out looking for similar ware, just a piece or two to fill out a shelf. For most of us there are never enough shelves.

While there are a few people quite willing to watch a collection grow without bothering to learn something of what they have, most find their pleasure in the old objects greatly increased and their skill in acquiring them much advanced by a little study.

The first and least difficult step is to obtain a book like this that provides general coverage of early American ceramics. Edwin Barber's *The Pottery and Porcelain of The United States* (New York: Putnam, 1901), is still a valuable reference work, as are John Spargo's *Early American Pottery and China* (New York: Century Co., 1926), and John Ramsey's *Early American Pottery and China* (Boston: Hale, Cushman & Flint, 1939). Although these volumes are, unfortunately, out of print, many libraries have copies. One can also pick up a little information in most of the general or survey-type antique books. Helen Comstock's *Concise Encyclopedia of American Antiques* (New York: Hawthorn Books, 1965) and a dozen similar works contain sections on pottery. Although these volumes usually provide little more than a general knowledge of the different categories into which early ceramics fall—porcelain, redware, yellow ware, and the like—this is important, since you now know what it is that is gathering dust in the front hall. If the acquisition is to your liking, you may decide to concentrate in that area. If you do, you will need to know the field in depth.

Assuming, for example, that you are collecting stoneware, the chances are very good that at least one of your crocks or jugs will be marked, i.e. will bear the name and/or address of the pottery where it was made. This is also true of American ironstone and porcelain. Roughly one piece of stoneware in ten and a much higher percentage of ironstone and porcelain were marked in this manner. Since relatively little redware or early yellow ware received the stamp of its maker, these areas require a different approach.

The marked ware is, of course, most readily traced and provides you with an opportunity to do some basic research. First, if available, you can turn to the general reference works. These, particularly Barber's *Marks of American Potters* (Philadelphia: Patterson, White & Co., 1904) and Ramsey's *American Potters and Pottery*, contain check lists of potters' marks, approximate dates of operation, and in some cases information on the potteries themselves. But they are survey books and do not, generally, contain the detailed information you are seeking. Also, these texts deal primarily with the craftsmen and wares of Ohio, Maryland, and the northeastern United States. They contain little information on the many clay workers once active in the South, Southwest, and Far

West. Until other areas are researched for books such as Lura Watkins' *Early New England Potters and Their Wares* (Hamden, Conn.: Archon, 1968) and my own *Early Potters and Potteries of New York State* (New York: Funk & Wagnalls, 1970), it will be necessary for you to do most of the work yourself.

If you have a marked piece you will find that this is not only feasible but extremely interesting. The usual post-1850 stoneware stamp contained the maker's name, hometown, and state: for example, DAWSON & SON/CAL-HOUN, MO. Porcelain and such whitewares as ironstone and hotel ware were marked in a similar manner or by use of initials combined with various figures—eagles, lions, and the like—which came to be associated in the public mind with a particular manufacturer. By referring to a listing of pottery marks such as Ralph M. and Terry H. Kovels' *Dictionary of Marks: Pottery & Porcelain* (New York: Crown, 1953), one can translate these cryptic designs into the name and address of a maker.

In either case, once you have this information it is a good idea to check the libraries' indexes to *Antiques*, *Spinning Wheel*, and similar publications. There have been many articles on various potteries in collectors' magazines, and the one in which you are interested may already have been written up. If not, the next step is to contact the state, county, or local historical society covering the area in which the artisan worked. Most public libraries maintain nationwide listings of these organizations. A letter detailing what you know and asking for further information will often elicit a voluminous and extremely helpful answer. It may, however, evoke nothing but silence or a demand for a stamped, self-addressed envelope. Historians are usually busy, unpaid volunteers, and the data you seek may be buried in books or files.

Thus, if the mountain has failed to come to Mohammed, the next step is obvious. If your local library has nothing much on the area in which you are interested, you must go to the source or hire someone to do so. Most libraries have lists of trained geneologists who would be qualified to research ware made in their area and would do so for a fee. It is cheaper and more satisfying, however, to do the work yourself. A visit to the appropriate historical society office will enable you to examine a variety of publications—directories, census records, local histories—all more or less pertinent to your inquiry.

The potter's stamp provides a name and a locality. A next step is to ascertain dates of operation. During the nineteenth century states, counties, and localities all issued business directories containing the names, addresses, and occupations of citizens. These also contained a smaller section wherein were listed the businesses of the area in alphabetical order, i.e. Ash Dealers, Asbestos Makers, and so on. Such directories should be checked both under the name of the potter on whom information is sought and under the headings Earthenware, Pottery, and Stoneware in the business guide. You may even be fortunate enough to find an advertisement placed by the man or company that made your crockery. At least you will learn when he or it was active.

The nineteenth century was also a period of documentation. Local histories and biographies detailed the past and extolled the virtues of living citizens. All these sources should be skimmed for reference to pottery makers. Since many of them rose to local prominence as aldermen, mayors, and such, you will occasionally find a complete life story of a craftsman and, perhaps, an engraving of his shop.

A third basic source of information is census records. Microfilm reproductions of the United States Census are available at most large libraries. From 1850 through 1880 they listed the occupations of all residents as well as age and country of origin, all valuable information for the researcher. New York, New Jersey, and some other states conducted their own census on the fifth-year basis, i.e. 1835, 1845, 1855. Film and often originals of these reports are in the files of many local historical societies and county clerks. Then, if you are really picky, you can turn to the recorded listings of births, deaths, and marriages to learn a little more about the craftsman and his family. Old newspaper files are also helpful in this regard.

Needless to say, the problem of attribution is much greater when dealing with a type of ware that does not commonly bear any written trace of its origin. A comparison of this book's photographs of Missouri, Pennsylvania, and Wisconsin redware shows similarities in style and manufacturing technique; yet these pieces were made at different times in different areas of the nation. The same is true of most yellow ware and Rockingham, a happy coincidence that has enabled many dealers to attribute any old spittoon or doorknob that happens to have a variegated brown glaze to the famous Bennington, Vermont, Rockingham manufacturers.

Regardless of what you may hear or read to the contrary, it is extremely difficult to learn the origin of most unmarked ceramics. There are, however, techniques that

Introduction

make it possible to draw reasonable conclusions in some cases. First, a certain number of unmarked items have come down with a reliable history. On the basis of family or former owner's information one can feel fairly confident as to their source. For this reason it is incumbent on the collector to spend what time he can in examining museum and private collections of early American ceramics. By observing peculiarities of style (for example, the unusual neck finish on the Wisconsin redware jugs shown in this book), coloration, and the like in a given potter's products, you obtain a fund of information which may make it possible to identify previously unrecognized work from his hand. Likewise, observation of such characteristics in marked stoneware helps to identify unmarked pieces from the same kiln.

In dealing with molded ware, such as Rockingham, however, it is not enough to note that marked and unmarked objects appear to have come from the same mold. Pottery molds were widely copied, were carried from shop to shop by roving potters, and were even swapped among manufacturers. This problem is magnified in dealing with utilitarian yellow ware where the extremely simple molds used for mixing bowls and the like make differentiation practically impossible. Accordingly, the history and background of a particular piece becomes most important here.

The identification of unmarked ceramics is a fascinating business, but it should not obscure the collector's interest in the ware itself. The beauty of an early redware teapot or blue-decorated stone pitcher is in no way lessened by the fact that its origin remains in obscurity.

Research and collecting go hand in hand. The person

who takes the time to learn something of the pots and jugs he is acquiring becomes more capable of locating and evaluating them. Certainly knowledge of local history, and particularly the background of the pottery in which one is interested, is helpful in determining where to look for new prizes. Due to limited transportation prior to 1850 pottery did not travel far from its source unless the kiln was located on a canal, a river, or salt water. Even after the middle of the nineteenth century local potteries, particularly in the South and Southwest, produced vast amounts of stone- and redware that were consumed within a radius of a hundred miles.

Accordingly, except in metropolitan areas, one can feel fairly certain that a perusal of antique shops, junk shops, auctions, and bazaars in the area of an abandoned pottery will produce a fair number of pieces traceable to the kiln. The educated collector will also quickly find that he operates from a position of strength when purchasing from these outlets. Few local antique dealers have detailed knowledge of early American ceramics (the very nature of their business requires them to have general knowledge of a variety of old things rather than specific knowledge of a few), and even fewer of the people who run bazaars and white elephant sales can tell a crock from a carboy. As a result the latter are excellent places to look for acquisitions, particularly of yellow ware and American ironstone.

In fact, if you collect these or even stone- and redware, you may find choice items in noncommercial settings. Much turn-of-the-century ironstone and porcelain is still in use, particularly in rural areas. A lot more is tucked away in closets and attics. Visits to a few friends and relatives may prove quite rewarding. The early collectors used to go through the countryside by horse and buggy, stopping at farmhouses to inquire about crockery. What they gathered became the basis of present museum collections. If you have the personality to do this sort of thing, it has possibilities. And while you are at it, check the barn, cellar, and outhouses. Stoneware is so hard to break up that it was easier to just tuck away somewhere. I once found a whole cellarful: shelf after shelf of cake pots, butter pots, jugs, and preserve jars, and in the middle of the room, great twenty-five- and fifty-gallon storage crocks still filled with cracked corn and grain. Even refuse dumps will occasionally yield an undamaged specimen.

How far one wants to go in exploration of these possibilities is a matter of personality. Some well-to-do collectors simply announce their needs to several prominent dealers and then purchase what is made available. In any case, there are still many fine early pieces available to the collector. It is just a matter of locating them—which is, perhaps, half the pleasure in collecting.

I

Redware

THERE is a wide range of clays available to the American potter. The most common of these are the red-burning surface clays found throughout the country, along the banks of streams and at outcrops on railroad or highway cuts. Flowerpots and common brick are both made from this earth, and for many years it was the basic material of the potter's craft.

Redware manufacture reached its height in New England and Pennsylvania during the eighteenth and nineteenth centuries, leaving behind a vast number of pieces, many of which are still available to the collector at reasonable prices. The type was also made in the South, the Midwest, and the Far West, but it is preeminently an Eastern ware.

TECHNIQUES *of* MANUFACTURE

The settlers of New England, New York, and Pennsylvania had a great need for common household ceramics. But earthenware is heavy, bulky and fragile. As a consequence, few families could afford to bring it with them

3

to the New World. Thus, since demand for ware existed and importation was limited, it was natural that craftsmen skilled in clay work found their way to the coastal villages. Early records are fragmentary; but by 1635 a Philip Drinker, potter, is recorded in Charlestown, Massachusetts, and Dirck Claesen was working in Manhattan in 1655. Little is known of these men or their contemporaries, and their output has long ago vanished.

In fact, examples available to the collector generally are of a far later period. Most surviving redware dates from after 1750 with the vast majority of pieces having been made in the nineteenth century. As a result, few collectors can expect to own pre-1800 examples. The focus of this book, consequently, is on the later, more common pottery.

The methods employed by the redware potter varied little between 1635 and 1850. Characteristically, the shop was run by one or a few men, often related. The product was always inexpensive, so costs had to be low. As a result the craftsman located within a few miles of a suitable clay bed. In the Autumn or Spring he dug out the season's supply and brought it by wagon to the shop. An underground cellar was used for storage.

As dug, the earth was coarse in texture, filled with pebbles and sand. After having been exposed to the weather for a month or so to achieve maximum plasticity, it was refined. The first step involved placing the lumps of clay in a shallow circular pit, lined with stone or wood. Into this extended a large wooden paddle that revolved on a shaft, crushing and grinding the clay into a single mass. Motive power for the device might be human or even steam, as in the later shops, but characteristically, it was a horse or mule who spent his days plodding in a circle about the mill, often bearing the additional burden of several neighborhood children grateful for their improvised merry-go-round. The animals employed in this manner invariably grazed in a circle when let out to pasture!

In later years the pit was replaced by the pugmill, a semicircular tank in which a shaft set with heavy knives revolved. In either case the end product was a puttylike mass which was then "screened" to remove foreign bodies. This involved forcing the earth through a wire screen at the base of a hand press called a jack, a vast improvement over the previous method of laboriously picking out the pebbles by hand.

Cleaned and reduced to a relatively even consistency, the clay was then cut into cubes or cylinders judged by weight or eye to be sufficient for a particular object. The potter was then ready to create. Near his house stood the work shop, usually a small, airy building with a few tables, a potter's wheel, and shelves for drying ware.

Some items were made solely by hand. The New England redware trencher or platter shown on page 90a is such an example. The craftsman cut out slabs of clay appropriate to the vessel and joined them by hand, smoothing over the joints. Pie plates were also often made this way.

For most of his work, however, the artisan employed the kick wheel, two horizontal discs joined by a vertical shaft. Turning the lower of the discs by foot caused the upper to revolve. A lump of clay placed thereon could, thus, be shaped as the potter desired. Handles, spouts, and

5

the like were usually shaped separately by hand and then affixed to the pot.

Other than the wheel, few tools were employed in potting. A few rib sticks or "smoothers" were kept about, thin pieces of wood with which to eradicate the "ribs," or ridges left on a pot's surface by the maker's fingers. There was a sponge to give a final finish, and perhaps a punch or coggle wheel for decoration. The latter was a little disc that revolved at the end of a handle, leaving a series of decorative impressions. By rolling the wheel around the neck of a vessel one might leave a band of identical stars or dots. Far more common was decoration produced by holding an awl or even a piece of stick against the side of the pot or jug as it revolved on the wheel. Skillful manipulation could produce the wavy multiple lines encircling the shoulder of the large New York preserve jar shown on page 90a. Such techniques were rarely employed after 1840, and mark a piece as being of uncommon interest.

The finished ware was cut from the wheel disc with a piece of wire and placed on a drying rack, where it remained for a few days until the surface was in proper condition to receive a glaze.

Pottery glaze is intended, regardless of its composition, to do several things: to strengthen and seal the object (*i.e.*, to prevent leakage), to give it a glasslike finish, and to decorate. In redware manufacture the problem of sealing is most important. Baked redware clay is relatively soft and porous. Liquids leak or "sweat" out, rendering the unglazed ware impractical for most purposes. Potters have known for hundreds of years that ground lead mixed with water and sand or fine earth produces a glaze that is watertight and durable.

Most potters followed the same procedure. Lead bought in bars or sheets was reduced to a white powder either by leaching in vinegar or by burning. The powder was then ground with the required amount of sand and water in a potter's quern or glaze mill consisting of two stones, a smaller top one fitting into a larger base. The ingredients were poured into a hole in the upper rock and emerged, crushed and mixed, from a smaller aperture in the base. The grinding, produced by turning the smaller within the larger stone, was another of the arduous tasks in the shop and was usually assigned to an apprentice.

The liquid glaze was applied to the dry, or "green," ware either by dipping the vessel into a bowlful or by pouring a quantity into the object and stirring it around. Bottoms were left untouched, since glaze there would have adhered in baking to the oven floor or another pot, resulting in damaged pottery.

After glazing, the ware was returned to the drying shelves for a few more days. Then it was arranged in the oven or kiln for firing. The potter's kiln was the touchstone of his art. If the process of baking proved unsuccessful, as it frequently did through lack of skill or proper materials, all the work that went before was wasted. Consequently, considerable thought was devoted to the most efficient oven design. The earliest, and the one which was used in the South and Southwest long after it had disappeared from New England, was the so-called groundhog kiln. This was a low brick or stone structure with an arched roof and a chimney at one end. At the other was an opening through which green pottery might be inserted. The ware was stacked and thoroughly surrounded with dry wood. The wood was then ignited and the entrance sealed except for air holes. The circulation within caused flame to pass across the ware, up and out the chimney.

Uneven burning was always a problem with this type of kiln, even when a firebox at the entrance end of the kiln was substituted for the random distribution of wood. Accordingly, at a very early date the Eastern potters began to employ a more sophisticated model. The total structure was much larger and built on two levels. The lower contained several fireboxes; the upper was the kiln proper, a substantial round or rectangular space in which the ware was placed. Flues to carry off fumes and smoke were also provided.

Packing the kiln prior to firing was an art in itself. Hundreds and even thousands of articles varying greatly in shape and size had to be placed in a relatively small area in such a way that they would not touch, for otherwise the glazed vessels would adhere to each other during firing. Pieces were generally stacked atop one another separated by flat slabs of unglazed baked clay called setting tiles. Also used were "cockspurs," tripointed pieces of the same material whose characteristic mark, three equally spaced dots, is often seen on the bases of redware bowls and pots.

When the maximum amount of ware had been placed within the kiln, the wood-burning fireboxes underneath it were ignited and the baking began. The fire was gradually built up in order to avoid the always present danger that too much heat too early would cause the ware to collapse. Fires were maintained for thirty to thirty-six hours, reaching a temperature of 1700° F. in the later stages. At this time the bricks of the kiln might turn white hot, only the iron bands that bound them preventing them from collapsing. Throughout the entire period the potter or his assistants stood by, feeding the fires from a handy wood supply and periodically removing test pieces to which wires had been attached so they might be drawn out through holes in the kiln wall.

At an appropriate time the fires were damped and the cooling period began. This usually took about a week, at the end of which the entrance was unbricked and the finished product removed. If all had gone well, the unglazed pieces such as flowerpots would be pinkish buff to red-brown in color (the higher the firing temperature, the lighter the ware color). The same would be true of the lead-glazed objects, since this common glaze was basically colorless. These latter, however, would be distinguished by a brilliant glasslike surface wherever glaze had been applied. The John Bell cream pot on page 90a is typical of this ware. It is unglazed on the outside, a form of economy for the potter who paid a fair price for lead, while the clear-glaze interior prevents leakage. The three Missouri pieces on page 90b bear a full exterior glaze. The preserve jar at the right clearly shows the absence of glaze on the base and upper rim, both areas of contact within the kiln.

While many craftsmen, particularly the later ones, were content with a clear finish, others sought to add color to their products. One way this might be done was through use of white clay, which, reduced to liquid form, was applied to the pot's surface prior to glazing. When fired, the piece provided an interesting brown-white balance. The trencher previously mentioned is an excellent example of this technique at its simplest. The redware body of the massive piece, fully sixteen inches long and weighing several pounds, has been broken into contrasting color planes by coating the interior with white clay.

More enterprising craftsmen employed a "slip cup"— (a clay cup in which several quills were inserted to serve as spouts)—by means of which multiple lines of liquid clay might be trailed across the ware body to produce varying patterns. The technique produced interesting effects, and ware so decorated was among the first to find its way into collections.

In Pennsylvania the use of trailed slip to decorate utilitarian pottery (particularly pie plates, whose flat planes lent themselves to the technique) reached remarkable heights of artistic expression. The Moravian potters of North Carolina were also early exponents of slip decoration, the platter by Gottfried Aust shown on page 90b being a fine example of the art.

The Pennsylvania potters also utilized the white slip clay in sgraffito decoration, a technique which seems to have been confined solely to the Keystone State. The surface of a piece of redware, usually the interior of a pie plate, was coated with slip. Then the craftsman would use an awl or some other pointed instrument to scratch an ornamental pattern through to the base clay. The baked piece would provide interesting contrast between the brown-red body and the yellow or white overcoat. Some of the most able potters worked freehand, but many artisans traced their basic sgraffito motif by use of a paper pattern, the outlines of which were punched into the clay with a blunt tool or pin. It was also common to use both techniques, slip decoration and sgraffito, on the same object.

This so-called Pennsylvania Dutch scratched-ware pottery attracted the attention of collectors before 1900, and there is very little of it outside museums and major private collections, despite the fact that representative examples were being produced as late as 1900. It should be noted that certain middle European pottery closely resembles this ware in form and decoration. If offered a piece, the collector is well advised to consult an expert in the field. At the very least one should examine the examples available at museums such as the Philadelphia Museum of Art or New York's Metropolitan Museum of Art. There is also an excellent discussion of these ceramics in Francis Lichten's *Folk Art of Rural Pennsylvania* (New York: Charles Scribner's Sons, 1946).

In New England, New York, and as far west as Illinois, potteries employed another mode of decoration, varicolored glazes, which were created by the addition of certain minerals to the basic lead glaze. Manganese oxide was widely used in the first half of the nineteenth century to produce a black metallic effect. Applied over the redware body it gave a sleek glaze much approved in tea sets. The "black teapot" was a standard piece in most country homes of the period. Similar vessels are still being made in Japan.

Various shades of orange and brown could be achieved by addition of iron oxide, which was generally prepared in the potter's shop. Pure iron was obtained from a blacksmith (red-hot horseshoes were an excellent source) and then burned in a sealed pot kept within the kiln. When an oxide state was obtained, the substance was ground to powder in the glaze mill. A similar procedure reduced copper filings to copper oxide and eventually to various shades of green-glaze base. The Massachusetts and Connecticut redware shops achieved remarkable combinations of blacks, oranges, greens, and browns, mostly on ware made prior to 1850. Potters farther west seldom worked with more than a single color, with the notable exception of those at Galena, Illinois. The eared flowerpot produced by this group, illustrated at page 90b, bears favorable comparison to New England examples.

Cobalt salts, which produced the blue used to decorate stoneware, were seldom applied to redware, since the color they produced on this ware was black, more cheaply obtained with manganese. A notable exception is the large redware crock shown on page 90c. This piece was made in Whitewater, Wisconsin, around 1850 and shows the strong influence in form and decoration of contemporary stoneware.

Simple earthenware shops produced a remarkable number of objects, both utilitarian and decorative. Manhattan's Dirck Claesen was making "earthen toys" in 1663, and whistles, marbles, clay banks, and the like were still being turned out by rural potters two hundred years later. Fat lamps and candle holders; a bewildering variety of household plates, pots, and jugs; inkpots, pen holders, and sanders for the desk—all these came from the oven.

From the earliest times some labor-saving devices were employed. The Pennsylvania potters utilized a crude mold for the making of pie plates. A slab of clay would be pressed down and over an unglazed baked form and the excess trimmed off. A slightly more sophisticated approach involved the use of convex molds whose interior bore a decorative pattern engraved in intaglio. Clay pressed into this form would emerge bearing a relief design. A "turk's cap" cake mold of this sort from the Perine Pottery in Baltimore is shown on page 90c.

In the last decades of the nineteenth century the dwindling remnant of the redware potteries concentrated primarily on the manufacture of flowerpots, and these almost without exception were mold made. By then little remained of the early handcraft skill.

I

The Eastern Redware
Potters

Most of the existent examples of eighteenth-century red
earthenware and the majority of all such pottery can be
traced to the band of states stretching south from Maine
to Pennsylvania. The first kilns were established here,
and the industry flourished in New England backwaters
until the end of the nineteenth century. There is perhaps
no ware that attracts the eye of the collector so quickly
as the multicolored glazed earthenware of this area.

Massachusetts

Though stoneware was produced in Massachusetts
before 1800, redware made from the abundant local clay
was always the staple item. Charlestown, near Boston,
was the early hub of this trade, and the potter Philip
Drinker was active here soon after 1635. His successors
were legion, nearly forty artisans being employed by
1750 at no less than eight different kilns. The volume of
pottery made here must have been very great. There are
records of its sale all along the coast from Maine to Long

Island, but no authenticated examples remain. This is largely due to the destruction of the town by the British during the Revolutionary War. Most of the craftsmen did not survive this blow. Only one, John Runey of Main Street, is known to have continued his business after 1800. His shop, founded in 1788, was carried on by sons and grandsons until after 1850.

At nearby Newburyport was another early shop, that of the Bayley family, earthenware potters from 1764 to 1799. Despite the antiquity of this pottery a great deal is known of Joseph Bayley and his family. The kiln site has been excavated by the historian Lura Woodside Watkins and a substantial amount of ware recovered including attractive cylindrical ale mugs in clear glaze, dainty earthen bowls and porringers, as well as plates, pans, chamber mugs, teapots, pitchers, jugs, crocks, and wash bowls. The Bayleys glazed much of their production with a variety of colors—mahogany brown, orange with brown streaks, black, and green. Objects such as deep dishes and porringers were often slip decorated, a popular combination being light yellow on yellow-green or brown.

Danvers was another great hub of the craft with over thirty master potters plying their trade there in 1800. The descendants of Joseph Osborn dominated the trade until mid-century. In later days the major proprietor was Moses Paige, who bought a shop in 1876 and managed it well into the twentieth century. His pieces, particularly clear-glazed herb pots, may still be obtained.

There were many other Massachusetts potteries. Lynn, Beverly, and Gloucester all had redware manufactories, as did the towns of Somerset and Berkley, where the Osborn, Shove, and Chace families produced crockery and storage containers brightly decorated with orange, brown, black, and green slip. These potters' shops eventually passed into other hands, and several were maintained until the 1880s; consequently, the ware, while scarce, may yet be found. There are several pottery dumps in Somerset, and excavation of these has revealed glazed ware including large numbers of red earthen flowerpots, many of them finished in a rich green.

In western Massachusetts there were important works at Northampton, Springfield, and Whately. A great deal of the earthenware produced at these and other Bay State manufactories has survived. Various Boston museums, in particular The Essex Institute in Salem and the Deerfield Memorial Museum in the western part of the state, have representative holdings. A fair collection, particularly of the late-nineteenth-century items, can still be acquired by purchase. Anyone entering the field for the first time should obtain Lura Woodside Watkins' *Early New England Potters and Their Wares* as a basic guidebook. Nowhere else is there assembled such a complete listing and illustration of Massachusetts, New Hampshire, and Connecticut redware.

Connecticut

While at one time or another probably every township in Massachusetts had a kiln, potteries, particularly of earthen- or redware, were less common in Connecticut. They also tended to be concentrated in major communities like Hartford, New Haven, and Norwalk.

Here, as in Pennsylvania, pie plates were a big item, an unusual type characterized by a notched edge similar to that found on like ware in the former state. Hartford was the great early center, with several shops active in the eighteenth century. The Wadsworth Atheneum, a major Connecticut museum, has a splendid collection, and antique dealers in the area stock an excellent though understandably expensive selection of redware, some of it documented as to origin. The Goodwin and Seymour families were particularly active in Hartford, the latter producing potters who worked later in New Haven, Troy, New York, and Ravenna, Ohio.

Prominent among the early artisans was Nathaniel Seymour, who built a pottery in West Hartford around 1790. He continued to make earthenware until at least 1825, utilizing native materials. The Wadsworth Atheneum has an excellent pitcher from this shop. It is a foot tall and richly decorated in light- and green-spotted slip on a brown background. There are also other pieces attributed to Seymour.

In the town of Goshen, not far from Litchfield, there were several early redware potters. The best known was Hervey Brooks, who moved there in 1795. Brooks plied his trade in the area from at least 1802 until 1867, leaving behind a substantial quantity of identifiable crockery including pudding pans, churns, pitchers, dishes, and bedpans, many of which were decorated with white slip. Brooks's pie plates, for example, are characteristically figured with a series of concentric circles and scallops in white slip.

Stamford had an earthenware manufactory in 1860. The firm of Wardwell and Gibson operated here for a few years, and there were other kilns in Danbury and Norwich. In the latter community Christopher Leffingwell was turning redware as early as 1771. The shop was later run by Charles Lathrop and the Potts family. Black- and white-slip-decorated red earthen crockery was made at this site until after 1815. Cylindrical preserve jars, pie plates, butter pots, mugs, pudding pans, plates, and bowls were among the more common items manufactured. The business never appears to have prospered, and after 1815 Norwich became a stoneware town.

In Norwalk Asa Hoyt and his son were running a pot- ter's shop in the 1790s, and the master craftsman Absa- lom Day worked there from 1793 until 1841, turning out a variety of lead- and slip-glazed redware. Asa E. Smith, a relative, made earthenware in the same community up until 1850, when it was abandoned in favor of stoneware. The Smith pie plates show the characteristic notched rim and a variety of slip decoration.

New Hampshire

New Hampshire had a large number of small potter's shops, the most successful being located along the sea- coast. There were potters in Portsmouth by 1720, and one eighteenth-century craftsman, Samuel Marshall, worked there for over twenty years. Joseph Dodge also ran a substantial works in the community from 1804 until at least 1839. Another Dodge, Samuel, was active in Exeter, as were Joseph and John Osborn of the Massa- chusetts potting clan.

Ware made in this state seems a bit more subdued than that of its western neighbors. Most glazes used were of a single color. Typical are the products of the Hampshire

Pottery in Keene, a late but successful manufactory that was established in 1871.

Representative of the men who toiled for many years at small shops in small towns was Daniel Clark, whose story is told in *Early New England Potters and Their Wares*. Clark was active in Lyndeboro by 1789. He worked later at Concord in a pottery run by his heirs until 1885. Ware made by the Clark family has been preserved at the New Hampshire Historical Society in Concord. Prominent among these are several marked pieces, always a rare thing in earthenware. Included in the collection is a brown-glazed ovoid jug inscribed MADE BY DANIEL CLARK IN LYNDEBOROUGH DURING THE YEAR 1792.

There was another family shop at Orange. Isaac Lowell built a small kiln there in 1818, and his descendants carried on the business until 1872. Examination of the old site indicates that the Lowells manufactured a great deal of redware, a few pieces of which have been identified, including a porringer, a cup, and a jug in the New Hampshire Historical Society collection.

Other New Hampshire manufactories were located at Boscawen, Plymouth, Canaan, Oxford, North Conway, and Chesham or "Pottersville," where rich sources of clay led to development of an extensive industry. David Thurston and Nathaniel Furber were making ware at Chesham in 1795, and by 1812 nearly a dozen shops were operating in the vicinity. The craft declined after 1820, but two manufactories (John D. Wight, *c.* 1845–60 and Eben Russell & Son, *c.* 1845–57) continued into the second half of the century. There is a good deal of ware attributed to Pottersville, but it is difficult to determine which of the many different craftsmen is responsible for a given piece.

Maine

Maine, like New Hampshire, was the site of myriad individual redware kilns. The Norcross family started to turn ware in Hallowell, near Augusta, in the 1780s. There were also pre-1800 potteries in Gorham, Wiscasset, and Yarmouth. Some establishments in the latter place were still in business in the 1880s, and pottery from there is on display at Boston's Society for the Preservation of New England Antiquities.

Many of the Maine works were extremely long-lived. The Kitson pottery in North Bridgeton ran from 1815 until after the Civil War, while Benjamin Dodge and his descendants founded a manufactory in Portland that made redware from 1801 until 1882 and continued thereafter in the stoneware line.

Dodge was a bit more interested in form and decoration than the average country potter. He made a large number of decorative pitchers, including one embossed with a representation of General Lafayette, and experimented with glazes, a trend continued by his son, Benjamin, who succeeded to the business in 1838.

There were other venerable pott works at West Farmington, Woolrich, and Monmouth. In the former community Josiah Norcross toiled from 1800 until 1869. John Corliss of Woolrich opened a shop in 1820, which was operated by others into the 1880s. Over fifty different potteries are believed to have operated in this state, and a substantial amount of redware remains, most of it unidentifiable as to specific source.

Vermont

It is much more difficult to obtain or even see examples of earthenware made in Vermont. Here the influence of New York stoneware workers and the availability of suitable clay (again from New York) early turned the craftsmen away from use of native soils.

At Bennington John Norton produced the familiar brick-colored crockery before 1800. A quarter of a century later he had turned to stoneware. A very few examples of his early work have survived. Included among these are vases, a milk pan, and a small black-glazed jug.

Moses Bradley of West Woodstock also made redware during the first quarter of the nineteenth century. Few of his jugs and storage vessels have come down to us. Some ware was also turned in Dorset by the Fenton family and at Middlebury by Caleb Farrar (1812–50). New Haven, St. Johnsbury, Chester, and Corinth were other shop sites.

New York

A similar situation prevailed in New York, where little is known of the pre-1800 earthenware centers. The earliest kilns were undoubtedly in the Hudson Valley, but with the exception of Selah Reeve at Newburgh, Amos Osborn in Pawling, and Joseph Shove in Hudson, few of the eighteenth-century craftsmen are known. Inland Joshua Starr was active from 1792 to the 1830s at

Cooperstown, but none of his production has come to light. After 1800 stoneware manufacture became dominant, and the men using native earth were confined primarily to the inaccessible areas, particularly the western frontier.

A few of these artisans survived late into the nineteenth century. At Bergholtz near Niagara Falls, Charles Mehwaldt made an impressive variety of earthen crockery between 1851 and 1885, some of which may be viewed at the Buffalo Historical Society. Lancaster, Leon, Lockport, Newstead, Jamestown, and Fluvanna all had redware manufactories, but little ware has been identified.

Fortunately, however, two of the western New York redware potteries marked their ware. The number of pieces which have been thus uncovered give one some idea of how much native earthenware may be masquerading as New England or Pennsylvania in origin.

At Morganville the Gleasen-Ford kiln was operated from before 1850 until the close of the century. Three pieces from this shop appear on page 90a. They show two characteristics of the later redware, the utilization of stoneware forms and the application of a clear glaze. Very rarely did the Morganville craftsmen depart from simple forms and minimal decoration. In fact, the tooled lines present on the neck and shoulder of the large crock can be regarded as unusual. The preserve jar on the left is unremarkable in form, being almost a direct copy of contemporary stone jars, but it bears an unusual black manganese glaze. A large collection of Morganville pottery has been assembled at the House of History in LeRoy.

Further east at West Bloomfield the Connecticut potter Alvin Wilcox manufactured a multicolored-glazed redware, which, if it did not bear the potter's name and location, would surely be taken for Connecticut or Massachusetts work. Wilcox was active from before 1830 until mid-century. A surprising amount of his work, primarily jugs and small pots, is known. A splendid example of the former in clear crackle-glaze is shown at page 90a. It is stamped A. WILCOX/WEST BLOOMFIELD.

New Jersey

Despite the abundance of stoneware clay and a thriving whiteware manufactory, New Jersey produced vast quantities of common redware. The Fulper Pottery, founded in Flemington in 1805, made glazed ware for many years before converting to stoneware and eventually to the whiteware still manufactured. George Hamlyn's East Lake Pottery at Bridgeton made similar crockery in the 1830s as did John Pruden in his first years at Elizabeth. Another Elizabeth redware maker was Andrew Forsyth, active in the 1860s.

One of the best-known nineteenth-century Jersey potters was John Mann, who turned out black-glazed redware teapots in Rahway from 1830 to 1900. Many of the Trenton manufactories also produced redware, particularly in their early years.

There were few towns in the state without a small kiln, and today western New Jersey is one of the few places where examples of common earthenware may be purchased at reasonable prices. A good collection of the early ware may be seen at the Newark Museum.

I / Redware

Pennsylvania

It is Pennsylvania, however, that may well be thought of as the "redware capital" of the nation. Nowhere else does this crockery exist in such abundance and variety. In the eighteenth century "Philadelphia earthenware" was sold and imitated throughout the colonies, and potters from this state played a major role in developing the clay-making centers of the South and West.

The German craftsmen of Montgomery, Berks, and Bucks Counties turned large quantities of slip- and sgraffito-decorated redware, most of which is today beyond the means of all but a few collectors. Among the better known artisans are David Spinner, an early-nineteenth-century Bucks County potter who specialized in freehand drawings of people and animals on pie plates, and Georg Hubener of Montgomery, a master of decoration and glazing. Both men and many of their contemporaries marked their products, often in flowing incised script.

As in other areas, of course, the majority of Pennsylvania pottery was neither marked nor decorated. Thousands of artisans manufactured plain unadorned household items, and even today certain types such as chamber mugs and cream jars are readily obtainable throughout the state. Most of these pots are not readily distinguishable as to maker; however, the Bell pottery in Waynesboro always followed the practice of stamping a substantial portion of its output, and for this reason Bell redware is much sought after.

The Bell family had a long and illustrious history in the craft, having owned or managed potters' shops in Maryland and Virginia. In 1833 John Bell, who had previously worked in Hagerstown, Maryland, as well as Chambersburg and Winchester, Virginia, built a kiln at the corner of Main Street and Leisterburg Road in Waynesboro. Here he manufactured redware and stoneware until his death in 1880. The small cream pot pictured on page 90a is typical of Bell's work and of most common Pennsylvania red earthenware. It is glazed only on the inside and bears the impression JOHN BELL. The original proprietor was followed by his sons John William Bell (1880–95) and Upton Bell (1895–99), both of whom continued the practice of marking their ware. In later years the bulk of the shop's output consisted of flowerpots, many of them glazed and decorated.

Another major Pennsylvania earthenware hub was Chester County, where dozens of different shops were in business during the nineteenth century. Kennett Square, where Edwin Brosius worked from 1846 to 1885; Westtown, the location of Isaac Esbin's kiln, c. 1849–54; and Oxford were all busy centers. Many of the Chester artisans carried on after 1900. The Grier Families' Mt. Jordan Pottery was turning out flowerpots as late as 1907, and William Scholfield of Honey Brook did not retire until 1927.

2

Southern Kilns

Redware was an early southern specialty but rapidly gave way to stoneware as the nineteenth century progressed. Today it is the more durable product that is thought of as typical of the area. The remaining specimens of Southern red earthenware are scarce and high priced.

Maryland and Delaware

Potters are known to have been active in Baltimore as early as 1764 and in Annapolis some eighteen years earlier. The Maryland Historical Society in Baltimore has a redware inkwell marked BALTIMORE/P. PERINE/1793, made by Peter Perine, Jr., whose son, Mauldine, managed a small earthenware manufactory into a corporation which remained active until 1938. The redware "turk's cap" cake mold from Mauldine Perine & Co. shown on page 90c is also from the Society's collection. In the same picture appears the unglazed clay form from which the piece was made. Molds of this sort were quite popular in the middle Atlantic states, and they are readily obtained in Maryland and Virginia shops.

Baltimore was a great potting center throughout the

nineteenth century, being exceeded in output only by East Liverpool, Ohio, and Trenton, New Jersey.

There were also many redware potters throughout the state, from Peter Bell, Jr., active from 1775 to 1824 in Washington County, to Martin Happel, who was still at his wheel in Hagerstown in 1907. Among the longest active were Jacob Lynn, who made glazed earthenware at Thurmont from 1853 to 1880, Joseph Bowman, working at Boonsboro in the 1860s, and Henry Scholfield of Rock Springs, who began to turn ware in 1861 and continued into the twentieth century. There is pottery traceable to all these artisans, and the most representative collection is in the Maryland Historical Society.

Delaware probably had a substantial number of redware works, though little is known of them today. William Hare (*c.* 1857–87), William Reiss, and A. Neumayer, all of Wilmington, are believed to have been earthenware makers around the middle of the last century. I have seen a few pieces, mostly in mottled green and yellow glaze, which are attributed to the area.

Virginia

In the Shenandoah Valley of western Virginia there was an earthenware center whose products are avidly collected today throughout the South and East. Strasburg had potters before 1830, and in 1833 Samuel Bell of the famous Bell potting clan purchased the kiln of one Byers. With his brother, Solomon, he continued the business until 1908.

Bell ceramics were normally covered with a cream slip then overglazed in green, red, and brown. Flowerpots and vases were popular items. As in Pennsylvania, marking of the ware was common.

There were other craftsmen in the community. Jacob Eberly managed his Star Pottery from 1880 to 1906, and Samuel H. Sonner & Son were active from 1853 to 1892. Other potters known to have made some earthenware were Amos Keister, who worked from 1850 to 1870, and J. M. Hickerson, who was in business from 1884 to 1898. Similar ware was made in Winchester by Peter Bell, Jr., who moved there from Hagerstown, Maryland, in 1824. He carried on his trade until 1845. Among his successors was Anthony W. Baecher, a German, whose ornately modeled and lavishly glazed pottery is in several museums. Baecher had trained in Maryland before coming to Winchester, where he worked from 1870 until 1889. Much of his work, particularly glazed vases and flowerpots, has survived.

North Carolina

The potting history of North Carolina spans two centuries and encompasses several traditions, not the least of which is that of slip decoration and sgraffito. The historian Stanley South and others have been active in reconstructing the history of the early Moravian kilns near Salem, but much remains to be learned.

The Moravian sect drifted into the state from Pennsylvania early in the eighteenth century. By 1756 they had a pottery at Bethabara, and this continued until 1802. The most famous of the master potters in charge of these works was Gottfried Aust, who was superintendent from 1756 to 1771. He went from here to Old Salem, where he toiled until 1788, using the large earthenware platter shown on page 90b as both a trade sign and a personal recommendation. This piece is both scratched and slip decorated, and its basic design of flowers, plant, and bird is reminiscent of Pennsylvania work.

Cream, green, and brown slip most often appear on Moravian pottery, and large pieces, particularly covered jars, seem to have been popular.

Aust was followed at Bethabara by his sometimes less than willing apprentice, Rudolph Christ (1786–89), and by Gottlieb Krause, active from 1789 until the shop closed in 1802.

Christ, in turn, was the supervisor at Old Salem from 1789 until 1821. In that year the kiln was turned over to a non-Moravian, John Holland, who ran it until 1843. The sect made stoneware as well as red and experimented with various whitewares.

By 1750, there were English potters in Moore County, the little community later known as "Jugtown," which has supported one or more members of the craft until the present time. The first of these is said to be Peter Craven, whose descendants abandoned the surface clays for stoneware and maintained a shop until well after 1900.

Kentucky and West Virginia

Kentucky had a variety of soils suitable for pottery making, and as early as 1796 John Carty and Ward Menelle were partners in a small earthenware shop at Lexington. Menelle departed in 1798, but Carty continued the business until 1845, by which time numerous other craftsmen had settled in the community. Though later superseded by Louisville, Lexington was the early Kentucky redware center. Unfortunately, little of the output has been identified.

Earthen pottery was turned at several other Kentucky communities, including Covington, where Cornwall Kirkpatrick, a Pennsylvania-trained artisan, ran a shop from 1839 until 1848. Kirkpatrick later moved to Illinois, where he was a partner in the well-known Anna Pottery. At Louisville the craft was established before 1840, and several redware makers, including George Keizer (c. 1840–45) and Abraham Dover (c. 1832–35) joined the stone- and yellow ware manufacturers in that busy potting town. No less than seventeen different firms operated there between 1829 and 1922. Red earthenware was also the specialty of A. J. Bauer, who ran a shop in Paducah, Kentucky, from 1886 until 1900, and Adam Cable, active at Hickman around 1860.

In the neighboring state of West Virginia there were at least as many manufactories. An early artisan known appropriately as "Master" Foulke turned out redware finished in yellow glaze at Morgantown from 1784 until 1800. He was succeeded by John W. Thompson, who soon switched to salt-glazed products.

Shepardstown also had an early earthenware maker, William McLuney, active from 1809 to 1813. He was followed by the Weise family, whose shop was opened around mid-century and lasted until 1880, when William Weise sold to the Happell clan, who continued the craft a few years more. Smaller but similar kilns were those of Robert Brown at Wellsburg, David Shorts in West Liberty, and Lewis Pierce of South Wheeling, all of whom worked between 1840 and 1860.

Florida, Georgia, Tennessee, and Mississippi

Stoneware products were dominant in the Deep South, with few earthenware manufactories after the first quarter of the nineteenth century. H. F. York of Lake Butler, Florida, is said to have made redware storage vessels from 1880 through 1900, and the large crock shown on page 90c is described as an example of "brown earthenware" made at his shop. In form the piece is closely related to stoneware made in the South during the same period.

As late as 1900 Georgia had over twenty separate potting centers, the heirs of a tradition going back to Andrew Duche, a Philadelphia craftsman who made red clay crockery in Savannah between 1738 and 1743. However, few if any of the later kilns manufactured earthenware, and I know of only a few pieces which may be attributed to the state.

Something more is known of Tennessee. While the early history is obscure, there were many mid-nineteenth-century kilns, several of which made red earthenware, or "dirt pottery," as it was termed in that area. Perhaps the best known of these artisans is William Wolfe of Blountsville, who manufactured slip-decorated redware from 1848 to 1878. A similar operation was carried on at the hamlet of Sulphur Fork by one Adam Cable. The Cable pottery ran from 1869 until 1875, and its proprietor was probably the artisan of the same name who had worked in Hickman, Kentucky, in the early 1860s. William Grindstaff of Happy Valley also made what he described in advertisements as "crockeryware such as crocks, jugs, jars, flower pots and tile" during the period of 1865 to 1888. Examples of his earthenware marked W. GRINDSTAFF are known.

At Biloxi, Mississippi, Joseph Mayer and his family produced some redware between 1856 and 1900, as was probably the case with several shops at Holly Springs.

Since there are quite a few pieces of earthenware attributed to the southernmost states, it is quite possible that further study by collectors or museum people will amplify what is now a sketchy redware tradition.

3

Midwestern Redware Shops

As the settlers moved west in the 1830s and 1840s, they encountered vast clay beds, particularly in Ohio and Illinois. The white stoneware clay of the former state provided an economic base for the nation's greatest potting community, East Liverpool. The red surface clays were found here too, however, and most Midwestern communities boasted a redware maker prior to 1850.

Ohio

In Ohio the Separatists' Society at Zoar employed potters such as Solomon Purdy, who made a wide variety of earthenware and roof tile. Samples of both may be seen at the Ohio Historical Society. The Zoar tile is particularly interesting as it is among the last and best representative of a ware type that was practically extinct by 1800. There are seventeenth-century records of tile potteries in New York and New Jersey, and the early Germanic settlers commonly roofed their houses with this material. By the nineteenth century, however, tile was generally discarded except in Pennsylvania and in Zoar, where it was made until the late 1840s.

33

I / Redware

This Ohio tile was handmade in wooden molds, the earth used coming from alluvial deposits along the nearby Tuscarawas River. Many individual pieces were decorated, either by designs cut into the mold or by freehand application of fluting, circles, and the like. The presence of initials and dates on some tile adds to the attraction this ware holds for collectors.

Though overshadowed by the later commercial potteries, Ohio's early redware kilns were most important to the expanding frontier communities. All the larger settlements could boast of one or more artisans. In East Liverpool John Koantz was turning domestic earthenware as early as 1817, and Joseph Wells remained active in the same community for thirty years (1826–56).

New Lisbon had several red earthenware makers in the first quarter of the nineteenth century, including Philip Brown and Oliver Griffith. Their output was primarily cups, bowls, and crocks, the very sort of thing most needed by the settlers.

Zanesville, later a great stoneware center, had an early redware potter, Samuel Sullivan, who arrived there around 1806. Though he had several followers, his art was not practiced widely in Ohio after 1840. By midcentury only a few common earthenware shops were still finding a market for their product. Chief among these were Constan Cook of Cleveland (c. 1859–68), and William Jenkins of Columbus (c. 1865). However, the brick clay still had some function. In the early 1880s it was employed by the Mount Sterling firm of Allen & Son in the manufacture of coffins!

Illinois

Illinois, like Ohio, was blessed with an abundance of white-burning earth suitable for making salt-glazed wares. A few small redware kilns grew up in various areas of the state, but at only one town, Galena, in the northwestern corner of the territory, did the craft thrive. Rich lead deposits were discovered here in the early nineteenth century, and by 1843 Eastern potters had arrived to take advantage of the glazing material available. The footed redware flowerpot illustrated on page 90b is an excellent example of their work. It is well formed and covered with a variegated-colored glaze distinctly reminiscent of New England pieces. A substantial collection of this unusual earthenware, including jugs, pots, and flowerpots, has been located through efforts of the Illinois State Museum in Springfield. Much of it is finished in mottled combinations of orange, yellow, green, and brown.

Best known, perhaps, of the Galena earthenware makers was Alfred M. Sackett, who was advertising "pottery of all kinds" as late as 1858. Ten years later, however, he was confining his output to stoneware, and the earlier branch of the craft was extinct in Galena. The influence of this community's earthenware workers extended beyond the state, however. Potters were trained here who later worked in Wisconsin and Missouri, and much of the Midwestern redware tradition may be traced to this spot.

Michigan and Minnesota

Even the Northern states, which lacked proper clay, imported the necessary means of making stoneware. As a result there were but a few earthenware kilns in the area.

Michigan potters were active as early as 1838, but no great amount of information on them has been accumulated. It is clear, however, that redware was being made in Detroit during the Civil War. Martin Autretsch worked there from 1863 to 1869, as did Theodore Blasley in 1865. At about the same period Aaron Norris was making pottery and tile at Marshall.

In Minnesota the major earthenware centers were Minneapolis and Red Wing. Louis Kampff established a pottery at the former city in 1857. Before 1860 his manufactory consisted of a log shack with a clay pit nearby. A stone building was then constructed, and the proprietor continued until 1876, when he sold to Jonas G. Swahn, who made flowerpots and terra-cotta ware until 1904. John C. Malchow ran the city's second earthenware kiln in the 1870s and 1880s, being succeeded by Julius Gobeaux (1895–1901).

Redwing's first potter was Joseph Pohl, who manufactured glazed redware crockery in a turf-roofed outbuilding on his farm north of town. A cake mold from Pohl's kiln is shown on page 90d. He made hand-turned butter crocks and flowerpots in the early 1860s, and was succeeded by William Philleo and Philander Sprague, who specialized in unglazed ornamental terra-cotta between 1868 and 1877. Several other men followed this trade in Redwing during the 1870s, but by the end of the decade stoneware had become dominant.

Other known Minnesota earthenware potters were Charles C. Cornell of Owatonna and Charles Rees of Elmwood, both of whom worked around 1870.

Wisconsin

Wisconsin's potteries, particularly those at Belmont and Whitewater, rivaled Galena, Illinois, in producing redware of the highest quality. The two small jugs from Belmont shown on page 90c are from the kiln of John Hammett, who was active between 1842 and 1879. They are in the collection of the Wisconsin State Historical Society at Madison. Both pieces are glazed in variations of yellow, orange, and green, colors also typical of Galena, where Hammett is said to have worked. However, form far more than color is the distinguishing characteristic of these jugs. The overall shape, particularly the neck and handle finish, is as stylish as anything ever done in this country. Hammett must be regarded as one of the outstanding nineteenth-century potters.

In the same photograph is shown a cream pot from Whitewater in a typical early stoneware shape and even decorated with cobalt, which, of course, turns purple-black on the red clay. Whitewater's first potter was Warren Cole, active from 1845 to 1855 (working from 1847 in conjunction with George Williams), and, from contour alone, it may be assumed that this pot is from his kiln, since ovoid pots were rare after 1850. Cole was followed by J. C. Williams & Co. (c. 1855–59), and finally, Dan Cole and Co., active until 1871. There was a second shop in Whitewater, this one run by Michael Ohnhaus and John Milz between 1859 and 1881. Although much of the glazed earthenware now found in Wisconsin must be attributed to Whitewater, there was another well-known redware craftsman, Konrad Langenberg of Franklin, who made teapots, cake molds, baking dishes, and crocks from 1860 until 1888. Langenberg's hand-formed Christmas tree ornaments are most prized.

Several Milwaukee shops made red earthenware, the chief artisans being Frederick and Albert Hermann, c. 1857–98) and John G. Bauer (1857–1905). The dominant product here was flowerpots, though household crockery was also manufactured.

Missouri, Kansas, and Nebraska

The westernmost midland bastion of traditional redware potting was Missouri, where the craft was introduced along the Mississippi River by French settlers. The first center was St. Louis, where George W. Ferguson and Christian Smith were making the ware before 1820. They were followed in the next decade by the firm of John Taylor & John Bradbury. No examples from these early kilns have survived.

After 1840 discovery of stoneware clay deposits led to abandonment of the red earth, and only a limited number of artisans, primarily in the eastern part of the state, pursued this branch of the craft. Most prominent among these were the Germanic potters of St. Charles and Hermann. In the former location Joseph Oser's kiln produced household ware in basic forms from 1847 to 1906. While coloring agents were occasionally added to the finish, typical St. Charles crockery bears only a plain lead glaze through which the orange-red body color shows clearly. The cream pitcher and preserve jars illustrated on page 90b are probably from Oser's shop. The taller jar is of a form most common in the Eastern United States. The other pieces show distinct local characteristics, most notable of which is the "squatty" profile.

At Hermann George M. Sohns made redware from local clays between 1846 and 1867. He was followed by a potter named Hoefer, whose output in the 1880s and 1890s was primarily flowerpots.

From Missouri west the number of potters' shops drops sharply. Kansas had less than a dozen communities where red earthenware was made. The largest works was at Lawrence, where Anton Grutz had introduced the craft in the late 1860s. A successor, the Schilling Pottery Works, employed sixty people in the 1880s. This firm, located on what was then New Jersey Avenue, had an extensive trade throughout the state prior to 1890. In Leavenworth Julius Keller & Co. made tile and utilitarian crockery between 1860 and 1863. At present no marked or otherwise identifiable Kansas redware is known.

In Nebraska, where surface clays were common, earthen flowerpots were manufactured in large numbers as an adjunct to the principle output of several stoneware plants. The Lincoln Pottery Works, which operated in the city of Lincoln from 1880 to 1903, kept twenty-five employees occupied in the 1890s and often produced a million flowerpots per year.

Another kiln, the Nebraska City Pottery, described its red earthenware as being of a quality that "would put to shame some of the Eastern potteries." Be that as it may, the firm appears to have lasted less than a year, and none of its output or that of other pre-1900 Nebraska redware shops is known.

4

Western Earthenware
Factories

Red-burning surface clays were common throughout the Western states and were widely used by the Indians. The Spanish who first settled the area continued this tradition, but their small local kilns have slipped into obscurity. Stoneware was dominant after 1850, and examples of the earlier product are uncommon.

Arkansas and Texas

Arkansas, particularly the counties of Dallas and Saline, produced a vast amount of common pottery in the second half of the nineteenth century. An increasing population demanded the ware, and geographical factors limited importation. While most of the craftsmen made stoneware, a few utilized brick clays. In Washington County a small redware business centered about the community of Cane Hill. William S. Crawley built a "groundhog" kiln here in 1846 and used native earth to make preserve jars, cream pots, and smaller objects until driven out of business by the great drought of 1874. During the 1860s there was a second shop at Cane Hill, this one owned by H. T. Caldwell & Co.

The Washington County product is said to have been salt glazed, and this finish was employed occasionally in the South for redware, though it was more commonly utilized for stoneware.

Eighteenth-century Spanish settlers introduced the potter's wheel to Texas, and the vessels manufactured were not unlike those presently made in Mexico. Redware, however, was not able to compete with salt-glazed pottery likewise made from local earth, and by the middle of the nineteenth century the latter was dominant. At least two potteries did continue the tradition. The Melcher shop at Weatherford in Parker County was turning out unglazed flowerpots as late as 1908, and at Elmendorf in Bexar County red clay storage vessels and agricultural ware were produced in the first decade of this century.

Colorado, Montana, and Utah

The mountain states had few potteries, a fact explained more by lack of population than absence of suitable raw material. There were, however, several clay-working centers in the region, one of them at Golden, Colorado. As early as 1871 Henry Bell was advertising his "Golden City Pottery & Firebrick Works" at the corner of Washington and Water Streets. The same vein of clay that supplied this manufactory today serves the American Clay Works and Supply Company of Denver, which was opened in 1893 by the Montague family. The latter plant has always produced red earthen flowerpots, first by hand and now through mechanical means.

Only one Montana pottery is known, the Busack kiln at Deer Lodge near Helena, which was in business from 1871 until sometime after 1875. The *Helena World Herald* of December 11, 1873, noted that:

> The pottery and redware works of Jack Busack, near the summit on the Mullin Pass, are being worked with good success. Mr. B. thoroughly understands all branches of the business, and experience has taught him how to manipulate the various clays with satisfaction.

Busack made pitchers, jars, jugs, platters, and flowerpots, including the large ornamental kind.

The pottery industry of Utah was of much greater dimension than that of its sister states, primarily due to the isolation of its Mormon inhabitants, who were for many years in a state of virtual warfare with the United States government. Forced to rely on native manufacture, Utah had a substantial number of small shops, no less than fifteen being reported in an 1875 directory.

In Provo a craftsman named Roberts built the first kiln around 1860. This manufactory, known as the City Pottery, was by 1871 in the hands of A. H. Bowen. Bowen's employees, two Danish brothers, E. C. and August Henrichsen, built their own works in 1872; and the former continued redware manufacture well into the twentieth century.

The lead-glazed red-clay milk pan illustrated on page 90d was made in Brigham City by Frederick F. Hansen, another Dane. Hansen was born in Copenhagen in 1833 and migrated to the United States at nineteen years of age, arriving as a Mormon convert and an apprentice to the master potter Nielse Jensen, at whose pottery in Salt Lake City he worked from 1852 until 1854.

In the latter year the young artisan removed to Brigham City, where he built an adobe house and kiln on First Street. After nearly twenty years of independent work Hansen was asked to establish a church-sponsored cooperative pottery. He undertook this task in 1874 and continued with his labors until the venture was discontinued. Like many other potters whose time had passed, he then became a farmer, an occupation he pursued until his death in 1901.

Hansen's redware bore a distinct resemblance to Eastern forms, and this well-shaped milk pan might have been made in New England a hundred years previously.

Salt Lake City had several potters' shops, including those of Frederick Petersen, active from 1852 until at least 1875, and the Eardley brothers, Bedsen, James, and John, all of whom worked there or at St. George during the 1860s and 1870s.

The Hyrum craftsman James J. Hansen, active from 1856 to 1909, left behind a substantial amount of earthenware, including bulbous cream pots and beautifully formed plates that are clearly modeled on pewter forms. Much of his ware has been preserved in private Utah collections. The same is true of the red earthenware made by John Eardley of St. George, Ralph Rowley of Fillmore, and Ephraim Roberts of Vernal.

California and Oregon

The Spanish made earthenware in San Francisco before 1800, but it was not until a half century later that the industry was established on a firm basis. East Oakland became the center with three manufactories—Daniel Brannon's Pioneer Pottery (c. 1856–87), the California Pottery, and the East Oakland Pottery—all of which made redware, mostly in the form of flowerpots and ornamental terra-cotta.

The California Pottery was a true pioneer enterprise. Started by the Edinburgh potter James Miller, the works first consisted of a single room, but by 1887 had grown to encompass three kilns and accessory structures. Miller's plant was still functioning at the turn of the century, then being known as the Oakland Art Pottery and Terra Cotta Works.

Terra Cotta, California, a settlement some ninety miles from San Diego, promised to become the flowerpot center of the West. However, after a high point in the 1880s and 1890s Terra Cotta quietly expired, leaving Los Angeles as the major producer of red earthenware, large quantities, primarily tile and pots, being produced there by J. A. Bauer and others. Several redware crocks bearing the Bauer mark are in private collections.

Oregon had a single kiln, that of S. H. Way, active at Eola between 1863 and 1868. Way was more than a potter; he was an innovator, though not a particularly successful one, judging from the brief life of his pottery. In 1868 the *Salem Daily Record* recorded its correspondent's visit to Way's premises, noting that the proprietor was

45

> ... such a man as the country is at this time most in need of. He is a great experimenter. He has discovered a kind of ochre, and also a kind of material which will answer the purpose of glazing. . . .

Way was succeeded at Eola by William Ramsey, Jr., who remained only until 1870. By that time the stoneware works at Buena Vista had usurped the market.

II

Stoneware

FOR most Southern and Western collectors the word pottery brings to mind common stoneware—the blue-gray or brown pots and jugs found today in countless antique shops, flea markets, and second-hand stores. The very durability that has insured the survival of so much of this ware was also the motivating factor in causing potters to work in this medium rather than local red clay, even when it was necessary to import the former from a distance.

Moreover, stoneware clay was raw material not so much for the individual village potter as for the small factory, and it as well as the techniques required for its use contributed in no small way to the industrialization of the potting trade.

TECHNIQUES *of* MANUFACTURE

In general the manner of making stoneware was substantially similar to that employed in redware manufacture, particularly in the South and Southwest, where techniques of the late nineteenth century were not unlike those utilized in the East a century before. Gathering, cleaning, and turning the clay were the same in both cases. The difference lay in glazing and baking.

Stoneware clay is a more or less white fine-grained earth which "reaches maturity," *i.e.*, is properly hardened, at around 2200° F., a much higher temperature than employed in redware ovens. The crockery produced at this temperature is markedly different from redware. It is much harder, steel hard in fact, and it is not porous, except where too much common brick clay has been mixed into the batch as an economy measure. This characteristic of imperviousness led in the earliest days to unglazed vessels, and a few of these have survived.

However, the typical stoneware was glazed, not with the minerals employed in redware manufacture, since these would disintegrate at high temperatures, but with common table salt, which was heated and then thrown into the ware-filled kiln when firing was at the maximum. The salt would instantly vaporize, covering the crockery with a clear, thin, pitted glaze not unlike orange peel in texture; hence, the term "salt-glaze" pottery. Stoneware finished in this manner may be readily distinguished by observation or by running one's hand across the surface.

Where not salt glazed, stoneware was coated with Albany, Michigan, or Texas slips, rare clays which, when mixed with water and applied as a finish, would fuse to a natural glaze at baking temperature. In the East and Midwest such slip was the customary interior finish, since the vaporized salts could not reach this portion of the vessels. The Albany-type clay mixture was also widely used as a surface glaze. In the North it was simply applied to the entire vessel, producing a brown coating, more or less lustrous depending on the temperature of firing. In the South the slip was employed in a more imaginative manner. In the Georgia jug shown on page 90e the potter sponged slip on in a flowing pattern, producing variations in shade not unlike those seen in the so-called Rockingham ware. A different decorative technique was utilized in the Florida vase on page 90e. There the craftsman used dots of slip to contrast with the buff ware body.

Another and very rare body finish was ash glaze, which was achieved by mixing alkali-rich wood ashes with fine-grained clay. Firing resulted in a soda-silica melt of remarkable attractiveness. A few such pieces are known, mostly from the South.

Decoration was always a problem with stoneware. Only two minerals, ocher and cobalt, could withstand the heat required for firing. The former was used in the eighteenth and early nineteenth centuries as a surface finish, most commonly appearing as bands of brown stain about the upper and lower thirds of salt-glazed Massachusetts crocks and jugs. After 1825 it was for the most part replaced by Albany slip, though occasionally used for interiors even after mid-century. Ocher was not, to my knowledge, employed as a purely decorative color, *i.e.*, in creating surface designs or highlights.

The typical stoneware decoration was achieved through application of cobalt, a dark blue pigment consisting primarily of cobalt aluminate. A general rule is that the earlier the ware the less color used and the cruder its application. Dabs of color at handle bases and crude flower designs or simply a streak of blue across the maker's stamp are typical of pre-1850 pieces.

In the second half of the century craftsmen developed a greater skill and versatility. Day schools and penmanship instructors were teaching a florid style of writing known as Spencerian, and among the forms to be learned by rote were animal and bird designs. Armed with this common school training, potters adorned their wares with a variety of freehand designs so faithful to the textual examples that motifs such as the blue bird, a popular collector's item, are remarkably similar from Maine to Ohio. These flowing blue patterns—particularly such inspired work as the Bennington, Vermont, deer and the Utica, New York, peacock—are among the finest nineteenth-century folk art.

As stoneware manufacture was phased out (from 1860 to 1920, depending on the area of the country involved), many larger companies employed stencils to achieve decorative designs on ware quickly and without need for a skilled painter. Cobalt brushed over a pattern (such as the frequently seen oak leaf of the Western Stoneware Company of Monmouth, Illinois) produced a pleasing variation in the surface. Few of these later adornments, however, can be compared with the freehand work.

Among the rarest of the cobalt-decorated pots are those that show a craftsman's individuality. Pieces bearing crudely drawn houses, trees, and figures or the well-written name of a local grocer all command high prices. Dated ware is particularly sought.

While blue was the dominant color, one will occasionally see a vessel adorned with brown-black manganese figures, either alone or in combination with the cobalt. Such ware is uncommon and generally fairly early.

Limited in palette, the artistic potter utilized, particularly in the early days, other methods to embellish his product. Stoneware more often than red earthenware bore coggle-wheel or punch patterns, etched lines, and in rare cases complete designs of ships, flags, and the like scratched into the surface prior to firing. These figures were frequently highlighted by the application of blue to the incised area. In some states, notably Pennsylvania and Ohio, stoneware table pieces were decorated by addition of embossed flowers, stars, and other objects, often enhanced by open-work designs.

The stoneware manufacturer had problems other than decoration, problems which directly influenced the course of the craft. First, the clay was not available everywhere and, hence, was generally more expensive. If one did not live adjacent to a deposit of suitable earth, it was necessary to have raw material shipped in by boat or wagon at substantial cost. Second, the higher firing temperature required more durable ovens. While "groundhog" kilns were used in Arkansas and parts of the South until after 1900, most manufacturers employed massive stone or ironbound firebrick kilns. These were of a permanent nature, unlike the typical earthenware furnaces, which might be disassembled after each firing.

All this meant expense, and one man could seldom finance a manufactory. As a result, stoneware shops soon became stoneware factories employing a dozen or more operatives. Individual skills in a part of the process, *i.e.*, glazing, throwing, or firing, replaced the all-around ability to pot.

This factor is one of the major explanations for the limited variety of stoneware forms. Where everything from dolls to coffins was made in redware, salt-glazed items rarely venture beyond jugs and a great variety of crocks. There are pitchers, beer bottles, and a few ink-wells and table pieces, mostly early, but the bulk of the output was restricted to the two basic types.

As the manufacture became limited in type and massive in volume (many nineteenth-century factories produced several hundred thousand items per year) labor-saving devices were introduced. Molds were used far more extensively than in redware potteries, and these were sometimes employed even in making jugs and crocks, which were traditionally thrown on the wheel.

Prior to 1850 the technique of throwing produced a jug or other vessel that was ovoid in shape, tapering away to both ends from a bulging center. Around mid-century the stoneware plants began to utilize "jollying," a technique whereby a vessel, while still turned on a potter's wheel, was formed in a plaster mold with scrapers being employed to shape the interior. The result was a straight-sided pot, the most typical stoneware form. As the most impressive cobalt decoration dates from the same period, it may be assumed that the new shape lent itself more favorably to painting. Since this was best done on a uniform background, the finest freehand work appears on large crocks that have been made from a mix of predominantly white clay. Such earth when baked shows a light gray surface on which the blue appears in striking contrast. Many shops, however, mixed red clays with the batch to stretch it, resulting in tan and even pink stoneware. The more local earth added, the less durable and waterproof was the product. In fact, if the mixture passed a certain point, the whole kilnful of ware might melt to slag above 1700° F. Economy, like virtue, has its risks.

Like redware, stoneware suffered a decline after 1875, largely due to the introduction of glass and tin storage containers. The craft did not, however, come to an end. Even today various Midwestern companies are making this ware, principally in the form of molded, mass-produced pots, crocks, and pitchers. Modern pieces usually have an undercoat of brown and white. They are seldom marked.

Eastern Stoneware

New York, Pennsylvania, and New Jersey were adjacent to the major Northeastern beds of stoneware clay, and they provide the majority of antique pieces found in this area today. New England lacked suitable native earth, and the expense of importation limited the craft, particularly in Maine and New Hampshire.

New Jersey

Vast beds of stoneware clay are found in the vicinity of Bayonne, and potters were working here well before 1800. Crockery fragments unearthed at the site of James Morgan's kiln in Cheesequake (1775–85) bear the dates 1775 and 1776. A second early shop was located at South Amboy, where the firm of Warne & Letts was active from 1778 until around 1820.

Another early workman whose ware has survived is Xerxes Price, whose pottery at South Amboy produced stoneware marked XP between 1802 and 1830. This town was a particularly active center for the craft, with several well known master potters busy there in the first quarter of the nineteenth century. Prominent among them were Joseph H. Remmey (*c.* 1820–23) of the Manhattan potting family and the firm of Humiston & Walker (*c.* 1826–35). All have left marked examples, primarily ovoid jugs and storage pots.

In later years the trade expanded to cover most of New Jersey, with the major centers being Newark, Elizabeth, and Trenton. B. J. Krumeich manufactured salt-glazed ware at the former community from 1845 until 1860, and a successor, the Newark Pottery, advertised in 1862 that its proprietor, John Osborn, "is constantly manufacturing stone and earthenware . . . of the best materials and latest styles which he offers on the most favorable terms."

At Elizabeth John M. Pruden and the firm of Pruden & Olcott made vast quantities of the salt-glazed product between 1816 and 1879. Much of this, particularly butter and preserve jars, is stamped with the address of the company's New York City warehouse, though the pottery was always located in New Jersey.

Smaller towns also had stoneware works, some of which, like Moro Phillips' Camden kiln (1867–97) and the Fulper brothers' shop at Flemington, were in business for long periods of time. The Fulper family began at the later location in 1805 and made stone pottery until well into the twentieth century, when they converted to whitewares. Much of their output was marked, and it is common in western New Jersey antique shops.

Other similar manufactories were A. J. Butler & Co. of New Brunswick (*c.* 1850), J. H. Peters of Red Bank (*c.* 1860–65), Van Schoik & Dunn at Middletown Point (*c.* 1860), and the pottery of Charles Wingender & Co., which turned out salt-glazed storage containers in Haddonfield around 1890.

Much late New Jersey stoneware was not marked, but sufficient variety exists to make for an interesting collection. Representative examples may be seen at the Newark Museum as well as at the New Jersey State Museum in Trenton.

New York

New Jersey was blessed with such an abundance and variety of potter's earth that her artisans soon turned to porcelain, yellow ware, and other products, leaving to New York the role of major Eastern stoneware supplier. That the need was met is evident from the almost universal presence of Empire State products. From Maine to Ohio and Virginia one finds pots impressed with the names of New York suppliers.

As early as 1735 the Crolius and Remmey families were running manufactories in Manhattan, and shortly after 1800 Paul Cushman in Albany, Nathan Clark in Athens, and Josiah Chapman in Troy founded potteries whose successors remained in business throughout the better part of the century.

Poughkeepsie had a stoneware maker at least as early as 1820; and after 1825, when the Erie Canal opened the western section of the state, major manufactories developed at Utica, Syracuse, Lyons, Rochester, Binghamton, and Buffalo. A collector may find marked ware from all these locations.

Fort Edward, in the northeastern portion of the state, was the site of four different manufactories producing a volume exceeded nowhere in the vicinity. There were also smaller shops such as those operated at Fulton, Sherburne, and Ogdensburg by various members of the Hart family. Shown on page 90e is a water cooler by William Hart, who worked in Ogdensburg from 1858 until his death eleven years later. Water coolers were among the larger early stoneware pieces and continued to be made right into the twentieth century. Here embossed bands and cobalt patterns enliven an otherwise rather prosaic form. Ogdensburg and Fulton were known for fine blue decoration, as were the Farrar Works at Geddes (1841–57) and the various potteries in West Troy on the upper Hudson.

New York pieces by Cushman and the early Manhattan potters command high prices, generally selling in the hundreds of dollars. There are, however, many fine examples by the upstate craftsmen available and at reasonable figures. The New York Historical Society, the Brooklyn Museum, and the Onondaga Historical Society of Syracuse all have extensive collections.

Pennsylvania

While Pennsylvania is known primarily for slip-decorated earthenware, stoneware clay was readily available, and there were a substantial number of manufactories. Salt-glazed crockery was already being made in 1810, when Henry Remmey arrived in Philadelphia to establish a family pottery that was to continue into the twentieth century. The early Remmey jugs, pitchers, and pots were of the same bulbous, lightly decorated nature as the family's Manhattan ware. After mid-century style changes were reflected in greater concern for ornamentation, and the work of Richard Remmey, owner of the manufactory in the 1860s and 1870s, is characterized by a profusion of rich blue flowers, particularly the tulip. This decoration was more popular in Pennsylvania than anywhere else, and unmarked stoneware bearing cobalt tulip patterns may often be traced to the state. Remmey products are highly prized and quite expensive. Fortunately, a substantial number are available for view in Philadelphia museums.

More readily obtainable is the salt-glazed crockery manufactured at Harrisburg by John W. Cowden and Isaac J. Wilcox. This enterprise was established around 1850 by Cowden and was a major stoneware source during the next thirty years. Much of the output was well decorated and marked either with Cowden's name or that of the later partnership. An ad placed in the 1867 edition of the *Harrisburg Directory* indicates the scope of this business:

HARRISBURG STONEWARE POTTERY
COWDEN, WILCOX & CO.
Manufacturers of
Stoneware of all kinds
including
Milk Pans, Fruit Bottles
ON THE CANAL OPP. CAR FACTORY
HARRISBURG, PA.

Pottery from this kiln is found throughout Pennsylvania and in New Jersey and New York.

There was an early stone pottery at Wellsville, where

Samuel Wells had a shop in the 1830s, and various smaller manufactories, including those of William H. Hill & Co. of New Castle (*c.* 1862–82) and Adam Burchfield of Pittsburgh, who made both stone- and earthenware in the 1860s.

Though perhaps better known for their redware, John Bell and his sons at Waynesboro turned a variety of salt-glazed wares in the second half of the nineteenth century. Their stoneware was fired to a bright blue-gray finish and was usually well designed.

Pennsylvania stoneware potters remained active into the twentieth century (there were three shops at New Brighton in 1907) and contributed a great deal to the development of the Midwestern industry. It was from here and from western New York that the first artisans were obtained for work in the Ohio kilns.

Vermont

Though the matter is in some dispute, better authority has it that the state of Vermont is lacking in proper stoneware clay. There were early attempts at making the ware from local material, but as early as 1810 John Norton of Bennington was bringing in New Jersey clay by wagon from Troy, New York, where it was unloaded from Hudson River flatboats. Nor was Norton the state's first stoneware potter. Jonathan Fenton, who had worked at New Haven and Boston, was turning pots and jugs near Dorset, Vermont, soon after 1800. His sons continued there into the 1830s, and there are a few pieces bearing the impression R.&C. FENTON/DORSET,VT.

Bennington, however, is the major source of marked

Vermont salt-glazed ware. From 1810 until 1893 John Norton and his successors owned manufactories in Bennington and East Bennington, and only in the later years could the production be regarded as less than substantial. The usual salt-glazed pots and jugs were made here, augmented by molded stoneware pitchers and similar vessels, glazed in Albany slip to resemble the then popular and locally produced Rockingham.

From 1823 on Bennington crockery was marked with the manufacturer's name, and collectors may roughly date their stamped pieces by comparison with the chart set out in the appendix.

There is, perhaps, more existent Bennington stoneware than any other, a fact which may be explained first by the unusual durability of the product (it was steel-hard, high-fired New Jersey clay) and second by the excellent quality of decoration. This was one of the first manufactories to use cobalt not simply as a highlight but in the preparation of intricate animal and plant designs. A large collection of this ware may be seen at the Bennington Museum, and most Eastern collections have a few pieces. Antique shows and shops often have examples, particularly of the most common, E. & L.P. NORTON.

Vermont had several other manufactories, the largest being at Burlington and St. Johnsbury. In the former community several proprietors were active at the same kiln from 1854 until 1895. The most common marks are BALLARD & BROS./BURLINGTON, VT., A.K. BALLARD/BURLINGTON, VT., and F. WOODWORTH/BURLINGTON, VT.

At St. Johnsbury Richard Fenton built a shop in 1808. His successors introduced stoneware, which was made there until 1859. There were also manufactories at Fairfax and St. Albans.

Massachusetts and Connecticut

The coastal states, though sharing New England's lack of suitable earth for stoneware production, were at least presented with the possibility of importation by sea. As early as 1743 some of the product was burned in Boston, and the neighborhood saw several other attempts before 1800, all of which were frustrated by the expense of transporting raw material.

At the very beginning of the nineteenth century, there appeared a variety of ocher-stained stoneware (mostly crocks and jugs) marked BOSTON or BOSTON, 1804. It is believed that some of these pieces were made by Jonathan Fenton, active in Boston in the late 1790s. By 1812 the Edmands pottery, most famous of the early Massachusetts works, had been established in the suburb of Charlestown. During the next ninety-seven years this kiln turned out a variety of ware, some of which rivaled Bennington in terms of decorative effect achieved. Common marks are B. EDMANDS/CHARLESTOWN and BARNABAS EDMANDS & CO./CHARLESTOWN.

Taunton had an active manufactory in the second half of the nineteenth century. Its ware, particularly that marked F.T. WRIGHT & SON, TAUNTON, MASS., is found throughout New England. There was a similar plant in Somerset operated by the Chace family from 1847 until about 1909. In nearby Worcester, the Norton-Hancock pottery was active from 1858 until 1885. Other Massachusetts stoneware works were located at Ashfield, Andover, Dorcester, and Whately.

In Connecticut Adam States established a stoneware kiln in 1750. His successor, Abraham Mead, ran the business until 1791. There were other early shops at Norwich, the best known being that of Armstrong & Wentworth and the Norwich Pottery Works, founded in 1835 and continuing to 1895.

The major stoneware-making center, however, was in Norwalk, where from 1825 Asa E. Smith and family manufactured a good grade of ware that was sold all along the Atlantic Coast. The firm had a Manhattan office, and much pottery is marked with that address, 38 PECK SLIP, NEW YORK CITY. There was no factory there, however.

Hartford had a stoneware craftsman in 1805. His name was Peter Cross, and some fine bulbous pieces bearing his mark have survived. Other early capital city firms were Goodale & Stedman (1822–25) and Goodwin & Webster, a partnership which survived for ten years after 1830. The kiln remained in the Webster family until the 1860s, passing then to Orson H. Seymour, who continued in various partnerships until around 1890. A substantial group of pottery from Hartford may be seen at the city's Wadsworth Atheneum.

After leaving the Hartford partnership, Absalom Stedman made ware in New Haven during the 1820s and 1830s. His work is marked STEDMAN or STEDMAN & SEYMOUR/NEW HAVEN. There were several other short-lived firms here, as well as S. L. Pewtress & Co., which operated for some twenty years after 1868.

New Hampshire and Maine

The lack of suitable raw material, which had been such a handicap in Massachusetts and Connecticut, proved overwhelming in New Hampshire and Maine. The former state had but two manufactories, that of Martin Crafts at Nashua (*c.* 1838–52), and a smaller concern in Keene, which was opened in 1871 by Starkey and Howard, then transferred to different quarters in the same town until it closed soon after 1876. Ware from both localities is rather hard to find.

Maine supported a somewhat more viable industry. In 1834 Martin Crafts of Nashua established a branch kiln at Portland. The manufactory's main output was flowerpots, jugs, and pitchers, some of which were marked M. CRAFTS & CO./PORTLAND. The Crafts family were still making stoneware in 1841, but discontinued shortly thereafter, being succeeded in 1850 by John T. Winslow, whose descendants still manage the Portland Stoneware Company. This major manufactory was rivaled only by the Bangor Stoneware Company, in business from 1890 until 1916, under management of the Pierson family.

There were smaller shops at Gardiner, where Alanson Lyman and Decius Clark were active between 1837 and 1841, and at Farmingdale, where Francis Plaisted worked from before 1850 until 1874. Other parties continued the business into the 1880s. Marked crockery connected with both these shops has been located.

2

Southern Stoneware
Kilns

Southern stoneware manufactories may be compared to
the earthenware shops of New England both in techniques and management. Like the latter area (and unlike
New York, New Jersey, and Ohio, where the business
was often conducted in factories) the typical pottery,
particularly in the Deep South, was a one- or two-man
concern centering around a kiln, usually of the "groundhog" variety. The ware was distributed locally, and the
operation often continued well into the twentieth century.

Maryland and the District of Columbia

The major exception to this pattern was Maryland,
where stoneware manufacture was carried on in much the
same way it was in Ohio. Peter Perine, Jr., of Baltimore
was making salt-glazed vessels in the first quarter of the
nineteenth century, and the firm that his family founded
continued the line into the 1870s.

Another early pottery was that managed from 1815

until mid-century by the Parr family. In 1845 the following advertisement for this firm appeared in the *Baltimore Directory:*

MARYLAND POTTERIES
ESTABLISHED 30 YEARS
JAMES L. PARR, SUCCESSOR TO
MARGARET PARR FORMERLY DAVID
PARR. MANUFACTURER OF STONE
AND EARTHENWARE WATER FILTERS
EDEN NEAR E. BALTIMORE

William Linton, a former associate of the Perines', also had a stoneware shop in the city, active from about 1845 until 1867. He was preceded by James E. Jones and Company (1834–45).

In the second half of the century there were several similar manufactories, the major one being H. S. Taylor's Jackson Square Pottery, which made a variety of salt-glazed products, including crocks and water coolers, in the 1870s and 1880s. Lesser competitors were Peter Herman of Eager Street, who worked for about twenty years after 1850, and Benjamin Greble, who made both stone- and earthenware during the Civil War period. Examples of these and other Maryland manufacturers may be seen in the extensive collection maintained by the Maryland Historical Society.

The District of Columbia had at least one stone potter, Enoch Burnett, who was listed in the directories from 1853 until 1869. His shop was located on the corner of West Eight and I Streets.

Virginia and West Virginia

Just across the river from the Federal Capitol is the city of Alexandria. There was a stoneware kiln here before 1840. Its original owner, John Swann, sold to Benedict C. Milburn in 1841, and the latter's family managed the business until after the Civil War.

Richmond also had a manufactory, this one run by the Parr family after they discontinued in Baltimore. According to advertisements, their Richmond Pottery made "Best quality stoneware, such as jugs, pitchers, jars, milk pans, spittoons, bread risers, butter pans, churns and water jars." This shop was active in the 1860s and 1870s.

The smaller communities had local stoneware potters such as William Wolfe of Big Spring Gap (*c.* 1875–81) and Moro Phillips, who worked at Wilson's Landing in the 1850s, but in salt-glazed as in redware the major center of production was Strassburg. Samuel and Solomon Bell made a variety of stone vessels here, many of which were marked. The same is true of Samuel H. Sonner and Son, whose manufactory specialized in the product from 1853 until 1892.

In West Virginia the earliest stoneware manufactory was that of John W. Thompson and Son in Morgantown. The Thompsons were in business from 1800 until 1890, and examples of their work have been preserved in the Smithsonian Institute at Washington, D.C. Another long-lived kiln was the Donahue Pottery of Parkersburg, founded in 1866 and active well into the twentieth century.

Even Wheeling, known as a whiteware and porcelain manufacturing center, had its stoneware works, under the management of William Day. There were also shops at Columbus, where Schenk and Rocker worked from 1870 until the end of the century, and at East River, where the local establishment was Brown and McKenzie.

Kentucky

In Madison County, near the town of Bybee, or Portland, as it was once known, stands the pottery of Walter Cornelison, fourth-generation owner of what is one of the last local stoneware kilns in the United States. The Bybee pottery was established in 1809, and as late as 1905 was making utilitarian stoneware. The present production is a variety of decorative pieces bearing little resemblance to the pots and jugs of yesteryear. Although the output has changed, the manner of manufacture has not, and the collector who visits Bybee will find the pug mill, wheel, drying racks, and oven common to the nineteenth-century kilns. Observing these latter-day representatives of the craft is an experience that cannot be duplicated by reading or research, and a trip to the shop is strongly recommended.

Madison County has long been known for its stoneware clay and has had numerous other manufactories, many of them near Waco, where D. Zittel and Company was active from 1870 to the early 1900s. As late as 1922 Grimstead and Stone were manufacturing blue- and Albany-glazed stoneware half a mile east of the town.

The Waco potters customarily glazed their ware with a mixture of Albany-slip clay, red lead, and manganese. Such a finish was common in the South, where the smaller kilns could not reach the high temperatures required to mature stoneware. The lead-and-slip mixture helped to bind an otherwise uncertain surface. This problem did not arise in the great ovens of the Northern and Western factories.

Louisville has a long history as a potting town, and some fine stoneware has been made there, particularly the well-known pieces bearing the mark of the Melcher family, proprietors of the Louisville Pottery, and active as early as 1845. The Melchers eventually left town for the West, founding potteries in Illinois, Missouri, and Texas. The Louisville Pottery, however, was still turning out salt-glazed ware in the 1920s. Such vestigial remnants of the trade were unusually common in Kentucky. Pottertown, Bell City, and Paducah all had active stoneware kilns in the 1920s.

North Carolina, South Carolina, and Alabama

The Moravian potteries of Salem and Bethabara, North Carolina, produced stoneware, both glazed and unglazed, before 1800, and the tradition was continued in the state for many years. In 1897 no less than fifty small kilns were active, the majority of which specialized in Albany-slip-coated stoneware. Here, the finish was commonly known as tobacco spit.

Many of the early craftsmen concentrated in the vicinity of Steeds, the area known for decades as Jugtown. Best remembered among these rural potters were the various members of the Craven family, whose progenitor, Peter Craven, is said to have come into the valley around 1750. Members of the clan were still potting here in the twentieth century. Another Steeds kiln was owned by

James Fox, who was exempted from service in the Confederate Army in order that he might manufacture vitally needed medicine jars and telegraph insulators.

Other typical North Carolina stone potteries were those of the Hilton family at Hickory and the Coles shop in Seagrove (both *c.* 1890–1900) and the kiln of Thomas Rhodes at Lincolnton, founded in 1865 and operating until at least 1900.

To the usual array of salt-glazed crockery—pickle jars, teapots, churns, and the like—North Carolina added a unique item, stoneware tombstones in the form of inscribed jugs. The earliest remaining one is dated 1838, the most famous is that marked with the dubious tribute to a deceased spouse, SHE DONE THE BEST SHE KNOW'D HOW.

Like Kentucky, South Carolina has an active kiln, the Bethune Pottery, which has been in the same family for four generations. Opened in 1871, this shop still provides tourists and collectors with a view of the potter's art as practiced in the last century.

Perhaps the most famous type of Carolina stoneware, or at least that which has attracted the most attention, is the so-called voodoo head jug, a crude vessel usually salt glazed, and apparently made in imitation of a Negro head. Despite the uniformly poor workmanship displayed in such pieces, they have attracted a great deal of attention. The primary reason for this is that they are among the very few anthropomorphic works known to American pottery. One of the major sources of voodoo head jugs is believed to have been the shop of Thomas J. Davies in Bath, South Carolina. Similar jugs were made in other areas of the South, and a few have shown up in the Northern part of the country.

Alabama, like most of the Southern states, is rich in stoneware clay. The Cribbs family established a kiln in Tuscaloosa around 1829, remaining in business throughout the century. They also had a branch at Bedford from 1865 until 1890. Other shops were the McLean Pottery Company in Coosada (c. 1880–90) and the manufactory managed by J. W. Williams in Pegram during the 1890s.

Here again the trade continued to a late date, with craftsmen employed at two dozen different locations in 1903, including Adler, Roanoke, Bangor, Blount Springs, and Oxford.

Tennessee, Georgia, and Florida

There were a substantial number of manufactories producing salt-glazed crockery in Tennessee. The major center was at Baxter, where at least three potteries existed. The oldest was owned by the Lafever family, which made utilitarian stoneware between 1840 and 1900. During the last quarter of the nineteenth century two other potters competed for the local trade. These men were William Hedicaugh and Monroe Vickers. Storage vessels and flowerpots were the bulk of their production.

If one considers the large number of kilns once operated in the South and the relatively recent time to which many of them survived, it would seem that this area should be a fertile field for collectors. There are, however, very few pieces traceable, by mark or otherwise, to kilns south of Maryland and Virginia. Moreover, with the notable exception of the Florida State Museum, few local institutions have acquired holdings in this field.

It is to this museum that we are indebted for the handsome Georgia jug shown on page 90e. It is from the Meader pottery at Cleveland, Georgia. The Meaders had a kiln here from 1830 until after 1900, and during the last decade of the nineteenth century they also ran a similar shop in Leo.

This is a particularly well-formed jug, a transition piece reflecting the change from ovoid shapes to the flat-sided vessels of the 1860s. The use of "flowed on" tobacco-spit or Albany-slip glaze is typical of pieces from this area.

The Georgia back country boasted numerous potters' shops. Among the traditional centers were Gillsville, where the Hewell pottery and the kiln of J. C. Halcomb were both established before 1835. The former was still making salt-glazed ware in 1900. The latter went out of business in 1887.

Leo, where the Meaders opened a subsidiary manufactory in 1890, was an extremely busy place in the 1880s and 1890s. Local directories indicate that no less than seven one- or two-man shops were competing there at that time. Nearly as busy was Mossy Creek, with four concerns making crockery during the same period.

None of these shops could, however, compare with the pottery of Henry Stevens & Sons, who remained in business so long (1815–1900) at one spot that a town, Stevens Pottery Post Office, memorialized their efforts.

Illustrated at page 90e is one of the few known examples of Florida stoneware. It is from the kiln of M. M. Odom and Robert Turnlee at Knox Hill, Walton County. The vessel is perhaps best described as a vase, though probably used as some sort of preserving jar. The decorative technique is unique. Drops of Albany slip were spattered on the pot, then it was salt glazed. These two finishes were often combined in the South, though not in other areas of the country. Odom and Turnlee were active for a very brief period, 1859–60, and examples of their work are scarce.

3

The Midwestern Manufactories

In the Midwestern states a happy blend of suitable clay, good transportation, and expanding population resulted in growth of several major potting centers. Though redware was made at first, and commercial earthenwares later came to dominate the trade (even as they do today), salt-glazed ware was the prime product. In fact, by 1880 the volume of inexpensive stoneware shipped from this area had become so great as to drive many of the competing Eastern and Southern firms to the wall.

Ohio

East Liverpool was the center of the potter's craft, not only for Ohio but for the entire region. Much of the early ware was made elsewhere, however. Springfield had several shops before 1840, including Fiske and Smith, active around 1828, and Edwin H. Merrill, in business during the 1830s. In Newton Township Joseph Rosier was manufacturing salt-glazed crockery by 1814, and Daniel Fisk's shop at Cleveland was a substantial concern in the 1830s.

Some of the best-known examples from the early

period are on display at the Ohio Historical Society's various branches throughout the state. Numbered among these are crocks, jars, and jugs from the hand of S. Routson, who worked in Doylestown from 1835 to 1846, removing from there to Wooster, where he continued until 1886. Routson's stoneware was marked, as was that made by Edward Hall, a Tuscarawas County craftsman who was one of the best modelers of the period. Hall was associated with the shop of W. P. Harris from 1828 until around 1856, during which period he turned out some extremely well-formed pieces, including shaving mugs, butter pots, and unusual bell-shaped jugs.

By 1850 the factory system, which developed here more rapidly than it did in most areas, tended to concentrate stoneware production in the Liverpool area and several other major centers. Chief among these were Cincinnati and Akron.

Uriah Kendall was manufacturing salt-glazed products in the former city during the 1830s. His sons continued the business through the next decade, though yellow ware making became a more important branch of the business in later years. Another Cincinnati potter who abandoned stoneware for various earthenwares was George Scott, whose shop was active soon after 1840 and continued past mid-century under the direction of his sons.

At Akron the manufactory of Hill, Foster, and Company was opened in 1847. E. H. Merrill, who entered the concern around 1851, continued it until at least 1894. By that time three other proprietors had begun to make stone crockery here: H. W. Rockwell and Company, Johnson and Dewey, and Johnson and Baldwin. Although the second and third firms were relatively short-lived, H. W.

Rockwell and Company was maintained until 1890. Other well-known Akron stoneware factories were F. K. Knapp (1865–85), the United States Stoneware Company (c. 1885–1900), and Beecher and Lantz (c. 1863–83). These and other similar shops in the city have left marked ware, primarily storage containers.

The major producer in Columbus was Amon Jenkins, whose kiln on Front Street first opened in 1840. The original proprietor managed the business until 1864, when he was replaced by a son, William, owner through 1868.

Zanesville had several manufactories, the first of which was probably Howson and Hallam, a partnership dating to 1840. In the last quarter of the century Clark and Bowen's Zanesville Stoneware Company was a prominent source of utilitarian ware. Massillon, also, had manufactories, including the Massillon Stoneware Company (c. 1880–1900). Other major centers were Mogodore, New Philadelphia, Louisville, and Navarre, whose Navarre Stoneware Works was in business during the last decade of the nineteenth century.

Illinois

The fascinating stoneware pitcher seen on page 90f is an example of the unusual ware produced at the Anna Pottery in southern Illinois. In 1859 Wallace and Cornwall Kirkpatrick established a stoneware plant in the community, first bringing in clay, then utilizing their own banks.

While smoking-pipe bowls, tile, and firebrick were also made, the major and most spectacular production was ornamental ware in the shape of bullfrog-adorned cups, snake-wreathed jugs, and shoe-shaped inkwells. The pitcher illustrated here is one of their more conservative creations, a cobalt and white slip-decorated political souvenir bearing caricatures of President Grover Cleveland and some members of his Cabinet. It was made around 1885, some five years before the pottery was closed.

The Anna pitcher was, of course, molded rather than hand thrown. It is essentially a factory piece, as is the Albany-slip-glazed cake pot illustrated on page 90f. This was made at the pottery of John N. Stout in Ripley sometime between 1866 and 1887. In the use of embossed circles, stars, and rosettes, and particularly the bird figure which doubles as a top lift, this vessel is typical of the Germanic work seen most often in Pennsylvania and Ohio.

The first Illinois stoneware was made by an Indian, Michael Baker, who settled near Whitehall in 1839. Since then several dozen localities have had one or more kilns, with major concentrations at Ripley, Peoria, Macomb, and Monmouth.

The Western Stoneware Company, established in 1870 at Monmouth, manufactured a white-slip stoneware preserve jar with a bail top similar to that used on canning jars, which shows up in antique shops all over the West and East.

Joseph Jager's Peoria Pottery (*c.* 1864–89) also made great numbers of Albany-slip-covered stone crocks, many of which were carried into the Far West by wagon train. Ware marked PEORIA POTTERY has shown up as far west as Oregon. The Eagle Pottery Company and Macomb Pottery, both located in that city, were equally active in the 1880s and 1890s.

Iowa and Indiana

While some of the later manufactories, such as the Davenport Pottery and the Union Pottery Works at Fort Dodge, attained substantial size, the average Iowa stoneware kiln operated on a modest scale.

Typical of these local shops was that built near Coalport by William Welch. Welch had been a potter since the 1820s, first in North Carolina, then in Iowa, where he worked at Fairfield and Pella before building his Coalport kiln in 1847. A few years later he sold out, and the property was leased in 1860 by Thomas H. Smith and his son Cass. The Smiths carried on into the 1870s with the son doing most of the turning. The miniature pitcher, saucer, and bowl shown on page 90f are from the hand of this potter. The pieces are all of stoneware, rather heavily turned, and glazed with Albany slip.

Iowa had many different pottery towns, but few locations could support more than a single artisan. Exceptions were Boonesborough, Carlisle, Lowell and Fairport, which in the 1860s could boast of half a dozen different shops, at least two of which were still active twenty years later. Outside Lowell stands a large stone building that was once the main workroom of the Melcher Pottery, which was located here in the 1870s. A second manufactory, the Lowell Pottery, was in the same area. Both marked their products, and Lowell stoneware, typically glazed with Albany slip, alone or in combination with sponged cobalt, is widely collected in Iowa.

79

As late as 1900 salt-glazed pottery was being made at a dozen different places in Indiana. The largest plants were in Evansville, and foremost among these was the Evansville Pottery, owned by the Uhl family from 1864 until 1887. As early as 1866 A. and L. Uhl were announcing themselves in a local directory as "Manufactures of stoneware . . . smoking pipes, water & drain pipe" as well as stove flues and flowerpots. Competing shops were run by L. Daum and Sons, active throughout the 1860s, Vital Walz (*c.* 1865), Valentine Gallman, and A. M. Beck, a latecomer who made stone products during the 1880s.

New Albany had a kiln for some years after the Civil War. Its proprietor, William Keller, placed the following advertisment in the *Indiana State Gazeteer* for 1865:

WILLIAM KELLER
Manufacturer of Stoneware
Fruit Jars, Flower Pots and Stone
Water Pipes
Corner Upper 7th & Water Streets
New Albany, Indiana

Other major potting towns were Annapolis, where H. S. Atcheson worked during the period 1841–1906; Harmony, site of the Brown Pottery from 1869 until 1913; and Logotee, whose pottery was in operation for fifty years after 1842.

Though identifiable Indiana stoneware is not unknown, the field has been neglected, and there do not appear to be any public collections within the state.

Minnesota and Wisconsin

In the Northern area stoneware production was handicapped by a lack of suitable local earth and severe competition from the Ohio manufacturers. In Minnesota there were a few abortive attempts, notably those of Christian Dauffenbach at New Ulm and Charles C. Cornell at Owatonna. Both made salt-glazed ware with imported materials during the 1860s.

It was not until 1877, however, that a firm with sufficient financial backing to survive for some time was established. In that year a group of businessmen purchased the tiny and failing stoneware pottery of David Hallem in Red Wing. This plant soon became one of the nation's leading crockery producers. When local competitors arose, the most successful of which were the Minnesota Stoneware Company and the North Star Stoneware Company, they were absorbed; and the combine, known as the Red Wing Stoneware Company, dominated its field for many years.

A vast amount of marked Red Wing, including a variety of large storage crocks, was marketed and pieces are found throughout the United States. Unfortunately, the very techniques which led to commercial success—mass-production molding and minimal decoration (usually by stencil)—make much of the ware relatively unattractive. However, some interesting early examples are on display at the Goodhue County Historical Society in Red Wing.

The Red Wing Union Stoneware Company abandoned utilitarian ware for table settings in the 1920s and went out of business in 1967.

Milwaukee and Sheboygan were the stoneware centers of Wisconsin. The riverbank in the former city was once piled high with Ohio clay brought to serve the kilns of Charles Herman and Company, John B. Maxfield, Isaac Brazelton, and other manufacturers. The Herman firm was opened in 1856 and continued into the twentieth century. It was an extensive operation, producing in later years a half-million gallons of stoneware annually (Western shops measured output by capacity rather than by piece as in the East).

The only serious competition within the state was offered by the Sheboygan shops. Issac Brazelton had transferred his business there in 1855, and he was succeeded by Theodore Gunther, whose Eastern Stoneware Factory produced substantial amounts of crockery between 1862 and 1887.

Missouri, Kansas, and Nebraska

The owl and dog bookends and the snake jug pictured on page 90g are products of what might be called Missouri's golden age of potting. Stoneware was made here as early as 1839 (by A. A. Austin & Co. of Commerce), but it was not until the late 1870s that market and transportation combined to promote a flourishing trade. By 1880 Calhoun and Clinton in Henry County were producing 65 per cent of the state's not inconsiderable output. The vast majority of this was kitchen crockery: cake pots, jugs, churns, storage crocks, and the like. However, potters and customers alike were fascinated with the decorative ware being made in Ohio and the east. What Ohio made in Rockingham or porcelain, Missouri matched in stoneware. Lacking yellow clay and a true Rockingham finish, the artisans employed mold-cast stoneware and Albany slip. The results were fascinating if sometimes a bit overstated.

The snake jug, for example, sports an unusual grained surface clearly intended to create the impression of wood or earth as background for the multicolored reptile. This piece is probably from the hand of August Blank, who worked at both Boonville and California between 1880 and 1900.

The slip-glazed owl and cobalt-blue poodle are cast in much the same form as their Rockingham counterparts. The dog bears the stamp of the Underwood Pottery, managed from 1880 to 1891 by H. J. and Paul Underwood. The owl is from another Calhoun kiln. The community had half a dozen different stoneware manufacturers between 1870 and 1895.

Decorative ware was unusual in Missouri and in most of the states west of the Mississippi River. In fact, for most crockery the opposite case prevailed. Pots and preserve jars, which in the East bore elaborate blue decoration, were here uniformly dull, relying upon a maker's mark or incised capacity number to relieve the uniformly gray or brown surface.

Missouri was the westernmost outpost of mass production, and through the 1880s and 1890s its potteries supplied much of the stoneware used in Kansas, Oklahoma, and the Dakotas. The railroads brought in cheaper ware, however, and by 1910 the industry was nearly dead. An exception was the Evans kiln at Dexter, which closed in 1942 after a run of ninety-two years.

In Kansas the craft never really got a foothold. There

were few potteries, only one of which, Keller and Hoffman of Leavenworth, is known to have made salt-glazed ware.

Nebraska fared a bit better. The first stone vessels were burned here in 1859, while the area was still a territory. The firm of John Ziegler and Charles Eckhart at Dakota City made straight-sided butter pots marked DAKOTA CITY, N.T. At present only one of these is known, but there are surely others hidden about the state in barns and cellars.

Later in the century there was a substantial shop at Lincoln, where W. and O. V. Eaton ran the Lincoln Pottery Works from 1880 until 1903. The firm was mentioned frequently in local publications of the period and used as an advertising motif a drawing of a stoneware jug with the words LINCOLN/POTTERY/LINCOLN, NEB. printed within.

The Louisville Stoneware Manufacturing Company was founded in 1879 on the site of an excellent clay deposit. Under various managements it continued through 1893. Here again the production was substantial. There were other potteries in the state that utilized local earth, but they saw fit to convert it to tile and drainpipe rather than household items.

4

The Western Potters

There are white-burning stoneware clays at various locations in the Southwest and along the Pacific Coast. These provided the basis for a substantial industry during the nineteenth century, with many shops continuing into the present era. The mountain states, on the other hand, never had or never developed the resource, and I know of no stoneware from this area.

Arkansas and Texas

In 1843 the Bird brothers, William, Joseph, and Natheniel, built a "groundhog" kiln near Princeton, Arkansas, and began the manufacture of salt-glazed ware. Their trade continued here until 1874, but by that time the focus of the business had shifted to Benton in Saline County.

Benton's first clay worker was Lafayette Glass, who had learned the trade from a Negro slave, one of several skilled black potters known to historians. After the Civil War and several abortive attempts at other locations, Glass settled in Benton. He was active here until 1879, soon being joined by other craftsmen. Between 1869 and

1900 there were nine different potters' shops in the vicinity, all of them making stoneware of one sort or another.

The pieces pictured on page 90g are typical of this output and of Arkansas ware in general. On the left is a wall sconce, probably intended for flowers, and consisting of two acorns on a national shield. It was made at the Hyten pottery in Benton around 1880. The miniature churn is a toy or salesman's sample. It is glazed in Albany slip. This vessel is also from the Hyten shop. On the right is a common storage crock slipped in white clay (the so-called Bristol finish) from the kiln of W. H. (Bud) Bennett, who worked at Benton between 1890 and 1900. Both the churn and crock are typical of late Western salt-glazed ware; plain and unadorned save for the stenciled maker's mark and capacity numeral on the larger piece.

While Saline County made most of this ware, Texarkana, Paragould, Rector, and Story all had manufactories in the last quarter of the nineteenth century. The most prolific of these centers was Texarkana, where the Collins family was active in the 1880s and 1890s.

In Texas the industry was more dispersed and more extensive. Ash-glazed stoneware was being made here before the Civil War, and there was sufficient demand to support continuance of the industry into the 1920s.

One of the earliest kilns was established in Guadalupe County around 1870 by Hirum Wilson, an ex-slave who had learned the trade while in captivity. A salt-glazed churn lined with brown slip and produced at the Wilson kiln is shown on page 90h. It is marked H. WILSON & CO., one of the earlier known Texas potters' marks. The interior finish is Albany-slip clay or one of the equally satisfactory local substitutes such as Alazan slip, a clay dug from the bed of Alazan Creek at San Antonio. Wilson and other members of his family made jars, jugs, and bowls until the proprietor's death in 1884.

By this time Elmendorf, in Bexar County, had become a major stoneware manufacturing community. William Saenger established a pottery here in the early 1880s. By 1908 he was making and advertising storage vessels with a capacity to fifty gallons, an exceptional size even for Texas. The Saenger kiln was active at least up until the first World War as was the Star Pottery, also located at Elmendorf. The latter establishment was founded in 1888 by Ernest Richter, a former employee at the Saenger firm. After some twenty years of management Richter transferred his works to Newton, Weller & Wagner, who introduced the tradename Star Pottery Works in 1909. During the next five years this works turned out a variety of pottery including the unusual churn illustrated on page 90h. The use of iron fittings in combination with a ceramic base is interesting and, perhaps, unique. This churn, the Wilson piece and numerous other examples of Texas stoneware are in the collection of Georgeanna Greer of San Antonio, one of the very few people to undertake an extensive study of the relatively unknown Texas pottery industry.

The scope of this craft is yet to be recognized, but at least fourteen different towns—Atascosa, Athens, Cornersville, Denny, Denton, Elmendorf, Henderson, Lavernia, Loyd, Marlin, Strumberg, Tyler, Weatherford, and Winnsboro—are known to have had kilns. Denton had three firms at the turn of the century, J. Sublitz, A. H. Moss, and D. B. Dougherty, all of whom manufactured salt- and brown-glazed pottery. Perhaps the longest lasting of all these firms was the Meyer Pottery at Atascosa built by William Meyer and Frank Schulz in 1887 and still making flowerpots under the direction of William's son Gus as late as 1940. Slip from Leon Creek near the plant was employed in glazing to produce rich green and mustard yellow crockery, much of which bore the mark MFG. BY/MEYER POTTERY/ATASCOSA, TEXAS. Equally important was the Russell Pottery at Henderson, Texas, which specialized in giant stone tanks for ranch and industrial use. Due to the long continuance and large volume produced by these Texas plants there is quite a bit of ware still available to the collector, much of it marked or otherwise traceable as to origin.

California and Oregon

The Michigan Bar area of California has extensive clay beds, and stone pottery was made there by J. W. Orr from 1859 until 1896. The earth was also shipped to Oakland, where Henry Bundock's East Oakland Pottery utilized it from 1872 until the late 1880s.

In the southern portion of the state the firm of J. A. Bauer and Company included salt-glazed wares in its varied selection of earthenwares. The Bauer pottery was opened early in the twentieth century and continued into the 1950s, by which time an extensive plant with four kilns had been established.

The Charles W. Bowers Memorial Museum in Santa Ana has one of the few public collections of California stoneware and includes among its pieces large crocks marked BAUER and J.A. BAUER/POTTERY CO./LOS ANGELES that were used in curing olives.

Another late shop was the Los Angeles Stoneware Company, whose wares were also impressed with the company name.

Southern California salt-glazed pottery was customarily decorated with transfer print patterns, oranges, leaves, and the like. It does not appear that freehand cobalt designs were used here.

There were also manufactories in Alameda, Elsinore, Lincoln, San Francisco, and Sacramento, but little is known of their history. The Sacramento pottery, believed to be one of the state's first, was established by the partnership of Baker and Gasser in 1854. By 1860 it was in the hands of G. D. Clark, and the Clarks were still running a plant here in 1887. It is believed that stoneware crocks and pipe were made at Sacramento.

A bit more is known of Oregon, where the first stoneware was made by Barnet Ramsey, a partially blind Illinois potter who settled near Springfield, Oregon, in 1852. He built a kiln the next year and worked at it for nine years, removing briefly to Albany between 1862 and 1864 and finally coming to rest at Halsey, where he was active until 1868.

The stoneware vase or preserve jar on page 90h is from the Springfield period. It appears to be glazed with Albany slip or a similar clay and is in an unusual shape, more Indian than European in concept.

Only a few of Ramsey's works remain. The best collection is at the Oregon Historical Society in Portland.

A second and much larger manufactory was established in 1865 at Buena Vista, a landing on the Williamette River. In 1868 this plant was the largest in Oregon, and it was still productive in the 1890s. Ware from the kiln of Freeman Smith and Sons at Buena Vista was described in an early newspaper as of "a density and fineness that cannot be excelled."

The Smiths had a second shop in Portland from 1885 until 1896. Both operations were known as the Oregon Pottery Company. A competing kiln, the Pacific Stoneware Company, was opened in Portland around 1892. First known as the Pacific Pottery Company, it was incorporated in 1910 and remained in business until the 1950s. Both firms made stoneware chimney tops, flowerpots, vases, drain tile, and similar items.

Redware trencher or platter with white slip interior, New England, c. 1840; lead-glazed flask, New England, c. 1830; jug with multi-colored lead glaze, Alvin Wilcox, West Bloomfield, New York, c. 1840. *(Private Collection.)*

Redware pitcher, preserve jar, and crock, Ford Pottery, Morganville, New York, c. 1875. *(Courtesy of Leroy House.)*

Redware cream jar, John Bell, Waynesboro, Pennsylvania, c. 1860. *(Courtesy of Keitha Parnes.)*

Glazed redware cream pitcher and preserve jars, attributed to Joseph Oser, St. Charles, Missouri, c. 1870. (*Courtesy of Roy M. Stubbs.*)

Slip- and sgraffito-decorated redware plate, Gottfried Aust, Salem, North Carolina, 1773. (*Courtesy of Old Salem, Inc.*)

Lead-glazed redware flowerpot, Galena, Illinois, c. 1845. (*Courtesy of Illinois State Museum.*)

TOP: Wisconsin lead-glazed redware: cream jar, Cole Pottery, Whitewater, c. 1845–55; jugs, John Hammett, Belmont, c. 1850. *(Courtesy of Wisconsin State Historical Society.)*

CENTER: Redware cake mold and plaster form, Perine & Co., Baltimore, Maryland, c. 1850. *(Courtesy of Maryland Historical Society.)*

BOTTOM: Redware (?) crock, H. F. York, Lake Butler, Florida, c. 1880–1900. *(Courtesy of Florida State Museum.)*

Redware cake mold, Joseph Pohl, Redwing, Minnesota, c. 1860. (*Courtesy of Goodhue Historical Society.*)

Lead-glazed redware milk pan, Frederick F. Hansen, Brigham City, Utah, c. 1860. (*Courtesy of Emma N. Mortensen.*)

Redware mixing bowl, Connecticut, late nineteenth century. (*Private Collection.*)

Stoneware jug, Meader Pottery, Cleveland, Georgia, c. 1870. *(Courtesy of Florida State Museum.)*

Stoneware preserve jar, M. M. Odom, Knox Hill, Florida, c. 1860. *(Courtesy of Florida State Museum.)*

Stoneware water cooler, William Hart, Ogdensburgh, New York, c. 1860. *(Courtesy of E. O. Hart.)*

TOP: Stoneware political pitcher. C. &
W. Kirkpatrick, Anna, Illinois, c. 1885
(Courtesy of Illinois State Museum.)

LEFT: Molded stoneware cookie jar,
John N. Stout, Ripley, Illinois, c. 1870
(Courtesy of Illinois State Museum.)

CENTER: Albany slip-glazed stoneware
bowl and pitcher, Cass Smith, Coalport,
Iowa, c. 1880. (Courtesy of Iowa Historical Society.)

Missouri stoneware: snake jug, attributed to August Blank, Booneville, c. 1880; poodle, Underwood Pottery, Calhoun, c. 1880–1890; owl, attributed to Calhoun Pottery, c. 1890. *(Courtesy of Roy M. Stubbs.)*

Stoneware wall sconce and miniature brown-glazed churn, Hyten Pottery, Benton, Arkansas, c. 1882; stoneware storage crock, W. H. Bennett, Benton, Arkansas, c. 1895. *(Courtesy of Patrick Dunnahoe.)*

TOP RIGHT: Salt-glazed stoneware churn,
Hirum Wilson & Co., Guadalupe County,
Texas, c. 1870. *(Courtesy of Georgeanna
H. Greer.)*

LEFT: *White-* (Bristol-) glazed stoneware
churn, Star Pottery Works, Elmendorf,
Texas, c. 1910. *(Courtesy of Georgeanna
H. Greer.)*

BOTTOM: Stoneware vase, Barnet Ramsay,
Springfield, Oregon, c. 1855. *(Courtesy of
Oregon Historical Society.)*

III

Brownware and Yellow Ware

AS the nineteenth century progressed, widening markets and the influence of European-trained craftsmen dictated a change in direction for American potters. For many years English and continental artisans had been using clays that burned to a cream or buff and proved admirably suited to tableware. Far lighter in weight than stoneware but more durable than the red body common in the United States, this ware was recognized by and named for its color.

TECHNIQUES *of* MANUFACTURE

While treated separately by some authorities, brownware and yellow ware differ essentially only in degree of clay refinement and baking temperature, the lighter ware being, of course, the more highly fired. In each case the clay is of a particular sort, finer textured than red earth, less dense and vitreous than the stoneware medium. It is fired at a temperature somewhat above 2000° F.

The yellow clays may be and often were thrown on a potter's wheel. An example is the Nebraska vase shown on page 142c. This piece is lead glazed and differs from redware only in the earth used. It was, however, far more common to employ these earths in mold-made pottery. Eighteenth-century European molded ware of this sort is known, and the process was introduced here as early as 1830. In New Jersey and Ohio, where suitable soil was particularly abundant, there grew up a substantial industry devoted to the mass production of molded brown- and yellow ware.

The techniques employed were far more sophisticated than those utilized in the making of coarser bodies. The raw clay was first placed in a large vessel called a blunger or churn, where it was reduced by mechanical means (the yellow ware factories usually were water- or steam-powered) to a creamy consistency. It was then passed through a series of sifters or bolters, which removed grit and foreign substances. The batch was then allowed to mature or age in large storage cisterns until needed. When suitable, the clay was run through hydraulic presses to remove liquid and then forced into a wedging machine, from which it emerged in blocks of suitable size and consistency.

The molding of bodies was performed in one of two ways. The first, known as jigging, involved the stamping or pressing out of individual pieces. A "bat" or glob of clay was pressed into a plaster mold (unglazed clay molds were at first used but later abandoned in favor of the lighter and more absorbent plaster of paris), which was then fixed on a rotating table. An attached cutting tool was lowered and used to trim off excess clay from the spinning mold. The clay-filled form was next placed on a drying rack, where it remained until sufficiently dry to allow removal, usually about twelve hours.

An alternative technique, one generally used for "hollow ware" such as teapots, creamers, and the like, was casting. Here liquid clay was poured into plaster molds and allowed to set until a suitable volume adhered to the mold wall. The excess was then drained off and the adherent clay was allowed to harden before removal. In either case handles and spouts were then shaped and applied by hand.

The complete vessel was baked twice, the first or bisque fire being intended simply to harden the ware, which was then glazed, usually with a clear lead or alkaline mix, and fired a second time. Much brown- and yellow ware received no finish other than this clear glaze, which served to intensify the body color as does the clear glaze used on redware. The jelly mold on page 142a exemplifies this unadorned pottery.

Much more common, however, particularly in kitchen ware, was the use of white, yellow, brown, or blue slip, rings of which circled a bowl or pitcher and added a pleasant touch to otherwise mundane objects. Several of the bowls and covered vessels shown on page 142a are decorated in this manner.

Perhaps the most popular finish devised for the brown and yellow clays was Rockingham, a glaze employing manganese and/or various metallic salts to produce a surface which varied from dark brown to the sponged yellow effect known as tortoise shell. Rockingham-finished stoneware is not unknown, but the glaze proved most effective when combined with the buff-burning clays. The three Baltimore pitchers on page 142b are examples of the technique as applied to factory-made items.

Rockingham proved so successful that it was widely made and widely imitated in whatever local medium was available. New England redware potteries often advertised earthenware with a brown manganese coating as Rockingham, and in many areas the finish was imitated by application of Albany slip to a stoneware body.

Much Rockingham, and yellow ware as well, was molded in sculptural relief designs. The embossed teapots, doorstops, candlesticks, and pitchers of the former material come readily to mind. The Roseville, Ohio, mixing bowl illustrated on page 142a is an example of the same technique applied to a kitchen piece.

For today's collectors Rockingham and yellow ware stand at opposite ends of the spectrum. Examples of the former, particularly from Bennington, are avidly sought and quite expensive. Few pieces other than spittoons and kitchen bowls may be purchased at reasonable prices. The relatively small number of marked vessels are in even greater demand.

Yellow ware, on the other hand, is yet to be discovered by most enthusiasts. Except where confused with the thinner and more sophisticated English mocha, it is in little demand. A rich field exists here, however. Many forms are known: banded teapots and coffeepots, pitchers, jelly and cake molds, covered storage crocks and serving dishes, pie plates, and doorstops. Prices are low, and the choice is substantial. The simple, pleasing forms are at home with modern interiors as well as country kitchens.

If the field seems unchallenging, then one might collect only those pieces which bear manufacturer's stamps. So little of this vast production (spanning at least a hundred years from 1840) was marked that building a representative collection will require both time and money.

I

Eastern Factories

Yellow ware and brownware belong particularly to the East and Midwest. In these areas the first factories were built, and here the industry attained its height, not only at Bennington, Trenton, and Liverpool but also in countless small manufactories scattered from Massachusetts to Missouri. Though today largely replaced by white clay products, Rockingham and its early companions remain in the inventory of several major potteries.

New Jersey

Although practiced decades earlier in Europe, the techniques suitable to these wares arrived late to the United States. It is generally agreed that the first successful manufactories were in New Jersey, where John Hancock, an English potter trained at the Wedgwood manufactory, established a shop at South Amboy in 1828. His products were yellow and Rockingham wares, the same staples offered by David and John Henderson, whose Jersey City Pottery, opened in 1829, proved an early and formidable rival. Under various managements this kiln continued active until 1892. It produced a large quantity of molded yellow and brownware in a variety of designs, many of which were sophisticated variations of current architectural and furniture styles. Toby jugs, pitchers, and even spittoons were designed to fit into a room furnished in the Empire or the Victorian motif. A large number of Jersey City pieces have been preserved. Perhaps the most extensive collection is at the Brooklyn Museum in New York City.

Trenton was the main nineteenth-century center for this trade, with a large number of factories, including William Young and Sons, active from 1853 to 1879; the Glasgow Pottery of John Moses and Sons, a maker of Rockingham, brown, and yellow earthenware between 1860 and 1890; Millington and Astbury, founded 1853 and carried on by successors until 1900; and the Trenton Pottery, owned by Henry Speeler, James Taylor, and various other partners for some twenty years after 1852. Substantial collections reflecting the workmanship of these firms are available for inspection at the Newark Museum and the New Jersey State Museum at Trenton.

Many other New Jersey communities boasted of a yellow or brownware kiln during the second half of the last century. At Woodbridge the Salamander Works made Rockingham from 1836 until nearly 1850, numbering among its tablewares a substantial number of historical and patriotic pieces. In Elizabeth was the shop of L. S. Beerbauer, active from 1879 to 1900, and not far away, in Perth Amboy, A. Hall and Sons made both yellow and Rockingham ware in the decade after 1860.

South Amboy also continued active with two short-lived but highly regarded kilns, that of Abraham Cadmus, known as the Congress Pottery and in business only from 1849 until 1854, and the Swan Hill Pottery, managed during its most creative period (1852–54) by James Carr, who later established a very successful manufactory in New York City. Both these plants concentrated on tablewares, particularly bowls, platters, vases, pitchers, and teapots, all highly ornamented.

Not all of the Jersey artisans hewed to the line of current fashion. At Rahway William Turner manufactured the most basic items during the 1860s and 1870s, advertising himself in 1868 as a maker of "Rockingham & Yellow Ware & Drain Tiles." Simple mixing bowls, jam jars, and the like were the stock in trade at this and many other New Jersey kilns.

In fact, almost from the first, the brown and yellow clays served different purposes. While it is true that some shops, such as the Jersey City Pottery, utilized copperplate engraving to transfer black decorative patterns onto a yellow body, this medium was typically simple and unadorned. The serving- and mixing-bowl forms (a major portion of the inventory of most factories from 1870 on) were little different from eighteenth-century redware vessels. In fact, well-refined brick clay would serve equally well for this sort of container, as may be seen from a comparison of the red earthen mixing bowl illustrated on page 90d with any one of its yellow ware counterparts shown in this book. It was not until fairly late in the nineteenth century that the use of relief decoration altered this traditional severity of line.

As a consequence, yellow ware was, for the most part, spared the Victorian excesses visited on Rockingham. The brown clay had proven an excellent base for this finish as well as being a highly malleable earth. As a result it was pressed into molds representing all the current fashions from leaf- and flower-patterned serving dishes to mugs decorated with quasi-medieval hunting scenes. The brownware glazed in Rockingham came out into the dining rooms and salons; the yellow ware stayed in the kitchen.

Some of the Rockingham pieces, notably those of leading factories such as Jersey City's American Pottery and the Salamander Works, are in excellent taste and extremely attractive. In other cases the effect striven for was not achieved. Today, however, collectors have created sufficient demand that even the less satisfactory examples from the New Jersey manufactories command a high price.

New York

In Manhattan and Brooklyn, where there was ready access to the New Jersey clays, there were several successful manufacturers of Rockingham and yellow ware. James Carr, former proprietor of New Jersey's Swan Hill kiln, opened the New York City Pottery in 1856 and made both yellow and brown Rockingham until about 1865. In Brooklyn there were several smaller plants, including that of Cornelius Vaupel (1877–93).

Upstate, Rockingham was advertised by potteries in Poughkeepsie, West Troy, Fort Edward, Utica, and Syracuse. It was, however, often imported rather than locally made, or if manufactured, created through use of Albany-slip glaze on a stoneware body.

The main center was Syracuse, where William H. Farrar began to make both Rockingham and yellow ware in 1857. He was followed by Charles Manchester and Fisher Clark in 1868 and Thomas G. White the following year. All succumbed to competition of the Empire Pottery, established in 1868, and soon succeeded by the Syracuse China Corporation. The latter did not make these wares, and the business disappeared in Syracuse.

Among the finest New York Rockingham was that made in West Troy, where William E. Warner had a kiln from 1829 to 1852. Warner had worked in New Jersey, and in the late 1840s he began to make Rockingham with New Jersey clay. His venture was brought to a halt by fire in 1852. Among the rare marked examples from this shop is a splendid covered dish at the New York Historical Society.

Pennsylvania

Philadelphia was a major nineteenth-century earthenware center. Thomas and James Haig, whose father had founded a pottery there in 1812, made Rockingham and yellow ware until after 1900. Isaac Spiegel, Jr., carried on a similar manufactory on Brown Street from the 1850s until 1879; and James E. Jeffers, who had worked for the Carr China Company in New York, built the Port Richmond Pottery Company in 1868. He specialized in Toby mugs and cow creamers with Rockingham finish, items which were being made as late as 1901.

Best known of these Philadelphia manufactories was that owned by Abraham Miller. His Spring Garden Pottery on Callowhill Street made both yellow and Rockingham ware as early as 1840. An 1857 advertisement indicates a wide variety of items was produced, including the so-called tam o'shanter mug. After Miller's death in 1858 the plant was continued by employees.

There were also a few factories outside the capital city, chiefly in Pittsburgh and in Phoenixville, where Schrieber manufactured brown and yellow earthenware between 1867 and 1877.

Massachusetts, Connecticut, and Vermont

Other than the substantial and well-known manufactory at Bennington, Vermont, New England had but a few potteries producing brown and yellow earthenware. In Massachusetts the Somerset Potters' Works made the wares during the 1880s, and Homer Caldwell's East Boston Crockery Manufactory was advertising yellow ware as early as 1862. By 1869 the firm was in other hands and manufacturing both yellow and Rockingham ware. This company became the New England Pottery in 1876 and continued until 1914, but little of these wares was made in later years. In fact, identifiable examples are rare.

At Norwich, Connecticut, Sidney Risley turned out buff-bodied Rockingham from 1855. The work, mostly doorstops, creamers, and molds, was termed "agateware," a name intended to impress the buyer with the durability as well as the attractiveness of the product.

At nearby Norwalk was the area's most ancient yellow ware manufactory. As early as 1832 Noah and George Day advertised for apprentices "to the Earthen and Yellow Ware" business, and the Smith Pottery at the same place was manufacturing both yellow and Rockingham crockery between 1860 and 1870.

Bennington, of course, was the center, particularly in

regard to Rockingham and kindred glazes. Christopher Webber Fenton began in the early 1840s to finish buff-bodied stoneware with a clear brown glaze. In 1847 he started making plain yellow clay crockery for household use as well as to develop a mottled or "tortoise shell" finish for brown earthenware. Then in 1849 he patented the so-called flint glaze, whereby ordinary Rockingham finish was enhanced with yellow and blue overtones through use of metallic oxides.

All the Fenton techniques were employed in the United States Pottery, where from 1850 until 1858 a great variety of wares was produced through highly sophisticated factory techniques. Unfortunately the management's advanced production skills were not equaled in the field of distribution. Poor marketing techniques and a location far removed from buyers and clay source led to financial disaster.

Bennington Rockingham is, perhaps, the most sought after of all American pottery. Literally dozens of different shapes were made, including pitchers, teapots, bowl and pitcher sets, candlesticks, doorstops, spittoons, and vases.

Several marks are known: FENTON'S WORKS/BENNINGTON,/VERMONT; LYMAN, FENTON & CO./FENTONS/ENAMEL/PATENTED/1849/BENNINGTON, VT.; U.S.P. and UNITED STATES POTTERY CO./BENNINGTON, VT. Many unmarked pieces are also attributed to Bennington through tradition, form, or finish, though the similarity of molds used in various manufactories makes such determinations most uncertain.

There are several excellent books on Bennington ware including John Spargo's *The Potters and Potteries of*

Bennington (Boston, Houghton Mifflin, 1926); and R. C. Barret's *Bennington Pottery and Porcelain* (New York, Crown Press, 1958). Substantial collections are held by the Wadsworth Atheneum in Hartford, the Brooklyn Museum, and the Bennington Museum.

2

Southern Yellow Ware

Limited technology and absence of suitable clays minimized Southern yellow and brownware production. There were substantial manufactories in Baltimore, but there was little further south. Many kilns made what was advertised as "brown ware," but this was simply stoneware glazed with Albany slip or a similar substance.

Delaware, Maryland, and Kentucky

Delaware had at least one kiln. Abner Marshall of Hockessin advertised both Rockingham and yellow ware between 1859 and 1866. Only one example from his shop is known. It is an ornate Rockingham candlestick.

The major center, however, was Baltimore, Maryland, where several nineteenth-century firms specialized in these clay products. Edwin Bennett, a native of Derbyshire, England, and a potter who had worked in both Liverpool, Ohio, and Pittsburgh, Pennsylvania, built a pottery at Canal and Canton Streets in Baltimore in 1846. He was making and advertising both yellow ware and Rockingham as early as 1849, and soon after mid-century established his manufactory as the area's largest producer of brown and yellow clay products. By 1880 over a hundred men were employed at the five-kiln Bennett plant.

Yellow mixing bowls bearing marks of the Bennett manufactory are relatively common, and Rockingham from this source is highly prized. The three Rockingham pitchers shown on page 142b are all from molds designed by Charles Coxon, a renowned modeler and associate of Edwin Bennett. The hound-handle vessel with embossed hunting scene is particularly well formed. The use of natural forms—a branch for the handle, an acorn for a lift —displayed in the piece on the left is typical of Baltimore work.

The Bennett firm continued under various managements until 1936; and it made Rockingham, at least, until the turn of the century. Utilitarian yellow ware was produced much longer. Excellent examples of both are at the Maryland Historical Society in Baltimore.

The Lewis Pottery Company in Louisville, Kentucky, made yellow ware as early as 1829. While this effort did not survive beyond 1836, other firms took up the trade. In fact, in 1922 the ware was still being made there, at the Louisville Pottery. Very little that can be traced to the Kentucky shops has survived.

3

Midwestern Rockingham and Yellow Ware

Ohio

Brown- and yellow-burning clays exist throughout most of the Midwest, and are particularly concentrated in the area of East Liverpool, Ohio. The English potter James Bennett arrived there in 1839 and was soon followed by his brothers Daniel, Edwin, and William, but their experiments with the local earth were cut short by a flood that in 1842 destroyed most of the pottery complex. The town's first successful commercial yellow ware maker was probably William Brunt, whose pottery was opened in 1847.

After the Bennetts departed, Isaac W. Knowles removed the usable portions of their old shop to an area called "the hill" (he was obviously taking no chances on further flooding) and began to make Rockingham and yellow ware. The business prospered. By 1868 four kilns were in operation. The proprietor's son-in-law, John W. Taylor, and his son, Homer S. Knowles, joined the firm, and it became known as Knowles, Taylor, and Knowles.

Competing plants were absorbed, and despite several fires, no less than thirty-three ovens were in use by 1926.

Another early brown- and yellow ware maker was Jabez Vodrey of Staffordshire, who came to Liverpool in the spring of 1847 and in association with William Woodward and James Blakely built an earthenware factory. After Vodrey's retirement his sons established the Vodrey Pottery Company on College Street in East Liverpool. By the 1920s this firm could boast of three thousand employees and an annual output valued in the millions.

There were many other yellow and Rockingham ware manufacturers in the same area. As early as 1859 local directories listed no less than ten separate potteries, among them Croxall and Cartwright, Foster and Garner, and Knowles and Harvey, all of which made the yellow clay products.

In Liverpool was manufactured perhaps the largest piece of yellow ware ever known. It was a pitcher five feet tall that was used as a trade sign by Woodward, Blakely and Company. The vessel remained atop a roof peak from 1847 until 1857, when it was removed to the nearby Great Western Pottery Works. The trail ends there, but it is possible that the immense pitcher still gathers dust in some Ohio barn.

By 1867 there were at least twenty-five potteries in East Liverpool, and the frequent openings of new manufactories were social events celebrated with parties and dances attended by prominent members of the community.

The Rockingham made here rivaled the Bennington

and Trenton product, and marked pieces, never abundant, are eagerly sought. The Ohio Historical Society has the most impressive collection, including several pitchers bearing the impression of Harker, Taylor and Company.

Yellow clay was primarily transformed into kitchenware, principally bowls and serving dishes, most of which is unmarked. A few of the later potteries did stamp their ware. Particularly abundant are examples bearing the mark R.R.P. CO. of the Roseville Pottery Company. In 1901 this company, which already had two plants in the community, purchased a former tile works and began the manufacture of what was described five years later as "utility ware, including pitchers, bowls, toilet sets and cooking utensils." In the next twenty years a vast amount of marked yellow ware was produced. A typical Roseville molded mixing bowl is shown on page 142a. Similar pieces may be obtained in antique shops from New York to Colorado.

The mark WELLER is also common. Samuel A. Weller had two factories, one at Fultonham, built in 1873, and another near Zanesville. In the latter, established 1888, he manufactured family glazed goods. The Weller firm became famous for art ware, but its domestic output showed little originality. This was as much as anything a reflection of passing time.

As a general rule the earliest yellow ware is the best. Crudely molded and lightly decorated if at all, it has a distinct charm lost in later mass-produced vessels. The pre-1900 examples illustrated on page 142a might all have been turned on a potter's wheel. Economy of line and simplicity in decoration are evident in all. The bowl on the right (probably from New Jersey) is particularly nice, with two broad bands of white slip atop a smudged chocolate base, the whole balancing a turned foot. The other vessels shown are decorated in brown and white, the most typical combination being one or two white bands within two brown ones. The small jelly mold and the two pie plates are only clear glazed. The banded storage dish on page 142a is unusual in that its form does not often occur in yellow ware.

Ohio had brown- and yellow ware factories at several locations other than Liverpool. To Roseville and Zanesville may be added Cincinnati, Akron, Tiltonville, and Middlebury. In Cincinnati George Scott established the Front Street Pottery in 1846. Yellow and Rockingham wares were made here until the end of the nineteenth century. Edward Tunnicliffe, active in Zanesville during the 1840s, was a renowned potter, and many other artisans established themselves at smaller yellow ware works about the state.

Indiana, Illinois, and Minnesota

Jabez Vodrey, the well-known Ohio potter, spent the early days of his career in Troy, Indiana, where a major yellow ware manufactory was built in 1834 by the Clews family of Staffordshire. Encountering technical difficulties in molding and baking, the management recruited Vodrey in 1839. Some interesting ware was produced, but the venture was never financially successful, terminating soon after his departure in 1847.

A second and similar Troy firm was established in 1851

by the firm of Saunders and Wilson. They turned out Rockingham and common yellow ware until 1863, when the management passed to Benjamin Hincho, who continued the business into the 1890s.

A somewhat smaller concern was active at Brazil, Indiana, during the 1860s. In 1868 the proprietors, Torbert and Baker, announced via a business directory that they "manufactured a fine quality of yellow earthenware, with a capacity of 75 thousand gallons annually."

Bott, Hamersley, and Company conducted a similar plant in Richmond throughout the last quarter of the nineteenth century. Bowls, storage vessels, and tableware were the major products.

Other yellow ware centers were scattered throughout the Midwestern states. Christopher Fenton and Decius Clark of the Bennington Pottery established a factory at Peoria, Illinois, in 1859. The highly skilled artisan Daniel Greatbach, who had been associated with the partners in Vermont, was brought west to oversee the business. Employing molds designed or furnished by this renowned modeler, the Peoria Pottery produced a variety of Rockingham vessels including hound-handled pitchers, bar bottles, and mugs in human and animal shapes, and tableware such as creamers and pitchers. Yellow ware was also made. The proprietors' hopes for the production of a line of fine pottery were not realized, however. Following continual financial reverses, the shop was transferred in 1862 to Amos Johnson, who operated it through 1873 as the American Pottery Company.

There were several other communities where the craft flourished. In Ripley, Illinois, John N. Stout made Rockingham-glaze doorstops, foot warmers, and the like between 1866 and 1887. Carbon Cliff also manufactured brown- and yellow ware in the 1880s. Among the many fine pieces uncovered by the Illinois State Museum at Springfield is a sitting poodle intended as a bookend or doorstop and made at Carbon Cliff. In form and finish it is similar to the Rockingham made at East Liverpool.

In Minnesota there was at least one yellow ware pottery. The well-known Red Wing Stoneware Company added the line in 1893, continuing to make yellow clay tablewares until well after 1900. Some of these Minnesota pieces bear the trademark RED WING/ SAFFRON WARE.

Missouri, Kansas, and Nebraska

The westernmost of the central states were too far removed from the technical centers of yellow and brownware manufacture to produce a viable industry. In Missouri Albany slip was widely used to imitate Rockingham finish on stoneware, but only one true brownware plant was operated. From 1881 until 1885 James Post at Cape Girardeau made Rockingham in some quantity.

Brownware is said to have been made in Kansas during the 1890s at Fort Scott and Geneseo, but no examples remain.

In Nebraska potters shaped the yellow earth not in molds but on the traditional turning wheel. Shown on page 142c is a vase or preserve jar of yellow clay with lead-glazed interior and an unusual classic shape. It was made at Nemaha, Nebraska, from local earth by the potter Trule Stevens. Stevens burned several kilns of ware here in 1860 in cooperation with a partner named Shaw. He made another kiln load in 1861, then left the territory, probably for Kansas. The Nemaha jar is the only known piece of Nebraska yellow ware. It is presently in the collection of the Nebraska State Historical Society at Lincoln.

4

The Western Shops

California

While the industry may have existed in other Western states, only California can definitely be determined to have had a substantial yellow clay manufactory. In the Bay area Daniel Brannon's Pioneer Pottery at Twelfth and Seventeenth Avenues in East Oakland was the major source of Rockingham and yellow ware. Both lines were advertised in the 1880s. Since this factory could then boast of three kilns, the output should have been significant. I know, however, of no pieces directly traceable to Brannon's firm.

In the southern portion of the state there were several late-nineteenth-century shops. The Fourth Annual Report for the State Mineralogist issued in 1884 noted that "some little glazed yellow ware" had then been made in the state. This may well reflect the output of the two firms whose products are illustrated on page 142c.

The small yellow-glazed custard cup bears the base mark PACIFIC and was made at the Pacific Clay Manufacturing Company, which as early as 1884 had a factory near Elsinore, later removed to South Riverside in the vicinity of Los Angeles. The company was located at this latter address in the 1890s, and the custard cup probably is from that period.

Another major producer of yellow and stoneware was J. A. Bauer and Company of Los Angeles, established early in the twentieth century. A large yellow-glazed mixing bowl bearing the Bauer stamp is shown on page 142c. As recently as 1920 this company was making "a complete line of red flower pots, white stone ware, yellow bowls, crocks, vases and ollas." As a result, substantial numbers of marked Bauer pieces may be found, the majority of which are dated as of the twentieth century.

The California specimens are for the most part pleasing in form and color and are not readily distinguishable from similar ware made in the East and Midwest. While good private collections exist, California yellow clay products have thus far been substantially ignored by the state's museums.

IV

Whitewares

THE great majority of all pottery made in present-day kilns falls into one of the several categories of white-wares. The desirability of ware both lighter and more durable than the commonly used red- and stoneware was early recognized by European and American potters. White-burning clays were utilized in seventeenth-century Continental manufactories, and a similar shop is believed to have been active here in the 1680s. It was a century and a half later before the industry became viable. From 1825 on, roughly parallelling the rise of yellow wares, the various whitewares conquered the tableware trade. Today the most refined of these bodies, white earthenware, is found in every American home, primarily in the form of dishware and cooking utensils.

TECHNIQUES *of* MANUFACTURE

Whitewares are produced from refined examples of earth found naturally in the United States. In New Jersey, Ohio, South Carolina, California, and other areas there are banks of highly plastic white-burning clay which, when properly prepared, may be fired at a high temperature to produce an opaque, non-vitreous, more or less porous body. At an early date this soil was utilized in redware slip decoration, and for many years it has been the major industrial resource of the American ceramics industry.

The whitewares common in this country may be thought of as existing in a continuum of refinement from the dark and relatively coarse cream-colored ware to the highly developed chalk-hued white earthenware.

At the less sophisticated end of the spectrum is cream-colored ware, commonly advertised as C.C. ware and made by a large number of nineteenth-century factories as an improvement on the then popular yellow earthenware. It possesses the same relatively coarse texture as the latter, being distinguished only by a somewhat lighter tint, after firing, hence the term "cream colored." This body was customarily given a coat of clear alkaline glaze and used for domestic pottery, mixing bowls, pitchers, and the like. The forms and molds employed are identical to yellow ware, from which it is not readily distinguishable. A variant was Majolica, for which a somewhat finer yellow body was glazed in one or more artificial colors, often pastels and often quite inharmonious. Developed in the British Isles and made here after 1870, Majolica in the form of ornate figurines, flower vases, and candlesticks satisfied Victorian tastes by being both gaudy and functional.

In Europe similar clay was refined through removal of impurities and foreign matter, then fired at a higher temperature to produce creamware, which possessed a fine homogenous earthen body only slightly off-white in color. Delftware, with a multicolored tin glaze on a cream base, was being made there in the 1600s, and by 1760 the English potter Wedgwood had developed Queensware, a variation of creamware that was light enough in weight and feeling to serve as a cheap substitute for porcelain.

Creamware was made in this country on a limited basis prior to 1850, but it was in the last half of the century that it came to be widely used in decorative tableware, primarily platters, plates, and pitchers.

By this time there was another innovation in the craft, white earthenware, which, being further refined, possessed a chalk-colored body of great strength and durability. It had been developed at the American Pottery Company in Jersey City during the early 1840s.

Both forms were customarily embellished through decalomania, or transfer printing, whereby a pattern or picture engraved on copper was reproduced on the ware body by use of a tissue-paper medium. Initially it was possible to transfer only an outline, body color being painted in by hand. Within a few years, however, the process had been expanded to include a fully colored representation.

The English flooded American markets with transfer-printed cream and white earthenware bearing portraits of political heroes and views of major United States cities. Competing domestic manufacturers were generally priced out of the market until tariffs were raised in the 1880s. As a result there are relatively few early examples from American kilns. Shown on page 142d is one of these, a transfer-printed version of Pickett's Charge at

Gettysburg from the Bennett Pottery in Baltimore, Maryland.

White earthenware gradually pushed creamware out of the field, and this body is today the medium from which most standard tableware is made.

For some years, however, serious competition was offered by English and American ironstone china or granite ware. This pottery, also known as semi-porcelain (though lacking the characteristics of true porcelain) and flint china, is highly vitrified, non-porous, and of greater hardness and density than white earthenware. Its extreme durability, exceeded only by that of stoneware, has found it a continuing place in chemical vessel manufactory and other areas where a shock- or acid-proof medium is required. Its great weight has, however, led to gradual elimination from the tableware field.

During the 1870s and 1880s kilns, primarily in New Jersey, New York, Ohio, and Maryland, produced vast amounts of ironstone and semi-porcelain, a late 1880s refinement better known as hotelware and characterized by greater vitrification and somewhat lighter weight.

American ironstone products have always suffered from a form of ceramic colonialism. When first developed they were held in such low public esteem that manufacturers were compelled to leave their wares unidentified as to maker or to mark them with counterfeit representations of the British Royal seal, in order that they might pass for imports. Trenton, New Jersey's, Anchor Pottery resorted to this latter technique in marking the mixing bowl shown at page 142d.

The citizenry, however, seemed remarkably adept at detecting domestic manufacture, a skill which the foreign sellers abetted by stamping nearly all their ironstone with firm name and country of origin. Finally, partially in desperation and partially in reliance on an emerging system of tariff barriers, the American ironstone makers (led by an East Liverpool manufacturer who replaced his prior false crest with a new escutcheon featuring the American eagle rampant upon a prostrate English lion!) abandoned subterfuge, and with a "buy American" campaign captured a major portion of the national market.

Yet even today the curse remains. English ironstone has been collected here for years, yet rare indeed is the antiquary who fills his shelves with the American-made product. The potential for collectors in this field is very great. The large potteries at Trenton and East Liverpool turned out some extremely fine examples between 1860 and 1920. If the general grade is a bit below that of the English in color (tending to lack the attractive gray-white ground hue of the latter) and temper, the best pieces are very good indeed. Certainly the Syracuse-made pitcher on page 142e is the equal of any similar imported vessel. Moreover, there is a wide selection to choose from, the great majority of which bears maker's identifying marks and all of which is relatively inexpensive.

The whitewares from C.C. to stone-china were made in basically the same manner as yellow ware. The clays, of course, differed in composition (mixing of several varieties was common) and refinement. All types, without exception, were molded rather than thrown on a wheel, and the production center was a small factory complete with division of labor, time-saving devices, and advertising department.

Two types of ovens were customarily used: the bisque

kiln, in which molded ware was burned for some seventy hours to achieve a fairly hard unglazed finish, and the gloss kiln, in which the pieces were baked after receiving a glaze of feldspar, silica, lead, and borax. Where decoration, by decalomania or otherwise, was involved, a third firing was necessary.

I

The Eastern Factories

Several New England potteries attempted whitewares, but the major successful manufactories were located in New Jersey, New York, and Pennsylvania, the states having capital, skilled artisans, and most important, ready access to suitable clays.

New Jersey

Central New Jersey has rich deposits of white-hued earth. This was early recognized as a commercial asset and was shipped throughout the East as slip clay for use in redware decoration. Moreover, as early as 1685 the soil was being used in Burlington, New Jersey, for the manufacture of what was probably delftware. The proprietor of this pottery was Daniel Cox, and his foreman was one John De Wilde, who later worked in Manhattan. This shop may have been in operation for ten years, but none of the dishware has survived.

There were further efforts during the 1700s, and by the middle of the next century New Jersey was the major whiteware producer in the country. In the 1850s many of the successful Trenton yellow and Rockingham factories began to add a line of whitewares. Typical of these was the Eturia Works, which announced itself in 1865 as the "Manufacturer of IRONSTONE CHINA and QUEENSWARE, CLINTON ST." Opened in 1863, this manufactory, under the primary management of William Bloor and Joseph Ott, was a substantial producer of high-fired earthenwares until 1876. A nearby competitor was the Assanpink Pottery Works, owned from 1864 until 1879 by Henry Speeler and Sons. This plant was located on East Front Street in Trenton. Ironstone or granite-ware was its specialty, as was the case with Burgess and Campbell's International Pottery Company, in business from 1879 until after 1900. The latter's mark, IRONSTONE CHINA/BURGESS & CAMPBELL, is well known.

In fact, most of the later Trenton graniteware makers marked their products. Some, like the Mercer Pottery Company (1869–1900), which used the terms "semi vitreous" and "china," saw their product as competitive to true porcelain and did not hesitate to advertise it as such. Others employed false Royal seals in hopes of passing for the similar but favored English ware. The iron-stone mixing bowl shown on page 142d is an example. Made by James Norrise's Anchor Pottery, it is impressed with the British lion and unicorn, a device used from the founding of the firm in 1894 until 1898. Thereafter, until the kiln was sold to the Fulper Pottery Company in 1926, a circle enclosing an anchor was employed as a mark. Designed in the Gothic tradition and quite light in weight and feeling, this bowl is a good example of the pre-1900 American ironstone still readily available to collectors.

Other makers of semi-granite whose pieces may often

be found in Eastern antique and second-hand stores are the Eagle Pottery Company (*c.* 1882–98), Union Pottery Company (1869–89), and James Cook, active for five years after 1895.

Of course this more durable ware was only a part of the Trenton production. The Eturia Works advertised "C.C. Ware" in the 1860s, and the Glasgow Pottery, owned from 1860 until 1890 by John Moses and his sons, manufactured a similar line, as did Charles Coxon's Empire Pottery from 1860 through 1880. A finer grade of creamware was employed by the American Pottery Manufacturing Company for dishes decorated with transfer-printed scenes of American cities and bucolic locales. Many of the remaining examples from this pottery date to the two decades preceding the Civil War. A somewhat later C.C. and white earthenware producer was the firm of Rouse and Turner, active in Trenton from 1859 until 1892.

Several other New Jersey cities had whiteware plants, including Jersey City, Elizabeth (where L. S. Beerbauer made creamware from 1879 to 1890), Newark, and Glouster.

New York and Pennsylvania

The Empire State began whiteware production later than New Jersey and never attained a similar volume of manufacture. While Abraham Wilson of Manhattan advertised Queensware in 1789, his efforts were apparently unsuccessful. By the following year Wilson was making stoneware, and it was half a century later that the first permanent earthenware pottery was established. Not too surprisingly, the proprietor was a New Jersey craftsman, James Carr. His New York City Pottery, opened in 1856, began with Rockingham, produced Majolica in the 1860s, and from 1870 until 1888 manufactured substantial amounts of ironstone tableware. Bowls, platters, and plates bearing the impression J.C./STONE CHINA are well known and eagerly sought by collectors.

There were a few minor whiteware kilns in Brooklyn, but the other large New York firms were located upstate in Buffalo and Syracuse. At the former city the Buffalo Pottery (whose mark, appropriately enough, was a standing bison) made transfer-decorated white earthenware from the 1880s until after the turn of the century. Included in its inventory were ornamental plates that were distributed by merchants as premiums in give-away contests.

In Syracuse was the major upstate kiln, the Onondaga Pottery Company, organized in 1871. There had been a previous whiteware shop in the city, the Empire Pottery, active in the late 1860s and known for its "empire ware," a white earthen tableware. In 1871 the Onondage Pottery absorbed its predecessor and began the production of ironstone, modifying its techniques in 1873 to produce an equally durable but lighter variation known as white granite. Shown on page 142e are three examples of the latter, a transfer-decorated pitcher, cup, and saucer made for the Philadelphia Centennial of 1876. The exceptionally stylish pitcher is a forerunner of the porcelain that became the company's main product after 1886.

The Syracuse China Corporation, as it is now known, has continued to expand, and today it is one of the East's largest potteries. The earlier ironstone and white granite (hotelware) is readily available in antique shops and junk stores throughout the Northeast. OP. CO./SYRACUSE/ CHINA is, perhaps, the most common of several marks.

Pennsylvania had equally well-known whiteware centers. Perhaps Philadelphia was the most renowned of these. Alex Trotter had built his Columbian Pottery there in 1808, and he made high quality creamware table settings on South Street until 1813, when he removed to Pittsburgh, where he claimed with some justification that his Queensware pitchers, coffeepots, and teapots were "similar to those of the potteries in Philadelphia." Abraham Miller, best known for his Rockingham and porcelain, also made some creamware at Philadelphia in the 1840s.

The smaller communities also had their kilns. Thomas Vickers and his son advertised for apprentices at their Downington Queensware manufactory in 1809. This establishment dated to 1796, though the early production was limited to redware.

After the Vickerses ceased operations in 1823, Chester County artisans confined themselves to redware until the 1860s, when the Phoenixville Pottery began to turn out white- and yellow ware. Majolica was added by Griffin, Hill and Smith in the 1880s; and in 1894 the old plant was leased by E. L. Buckwalter and H. I. Brown, who made "black stamped, & Semi-granite ware, white and decorated ware, colored glazed ware in nine colors, in toilet, table and other pieces" until 1899. One of their semi-granite pitchers marked CHESTER/HOTEL/CHINA is shown on page 142f. It is typical of the massive ironstone then being made from New York to Ohio.

Next to the Chester pitcher is an egg cup from the

Shenango China Company, which was incorporated at New Castle in 1910. At times six kilns and 150 men were employed. The firm's most popular mark was a pipe-smoking Indian.

Beaver Falls also had whiteware potteries, some of which were established as early as 1834. The business continued until after 1900.

Massachusetts and Vermont

New England's production of whitewares was always quite limited. Massachusetts artisans attempted decorated earthenware in the eighteenth century, but little has been learned of this shop or its products. Many years later the state had a more ambitious works, the East-Boston Crockery Manufactory previously mentioned in connection with Rockingham and yellow ware. In 1862 the owners advertised themselves as "Manufacturers of China and Parian Ware, White Granite and Ironstone." This company ran, under various managements, until 1914. Ironstone table- and toilet ware, much of it marked N.E.P. CO., for New England Pottery Company, was made throughout this period. In the 1880s a cream-colored earthenware trade named rieta ware was manufactured as well as cream and white earthenware. Much of the output was stamped with the manufacturer's cypher. Boston's Society for the Preservation of New England Antiquities has numerous examples from this manufactory.

At Bennington Christopher Webber Fenton began turning out white earthenware in 1847, and much of the so-called flint-enamel ware produced there by the United States Pottery had a body composed of white clay from

Charleston, South Carolina. Also, in the early 1850s, Fenton's plant developed two varieties of ironstone, the heavy graniteware and a semi-porcelain or hotelware used in tea sets. These latter were seldom marked and can only be attributed to Bennington on the basis of form and history. An exception is the Saint Nicholas pitcher, a heavy ironstone vessel designed for use in hotels (the name refers to a hotel by that name in New York where these pitchers were widely used) and frequently decorated in green, gold, and blue. Saint Nicholas ware often bore the name of the purchaser and less frequently of the pottery.

Like all ware which can be attributed, no matter how remotely, to Bennington, this ironstone is exceedingly hard to obtain today. The best examples are in museums or in private hands.

2

Southern Whiteware
Potteries

The Southern states, particularly North and South Carolina, have an abundance of the white clays suitable for making fine pottery and porcelain. These were mined for export, even in the eighteenth century.

South Carolina and North Carolina

In 1770 the English craftsman John Bartlam established a shop at Charlestown, South Carolina, where he attempted to produce Queensware (creamware) with a group of Staffordshire workmen. Disease carried off most of his employees, and the experiment is not believed to have lasted more than two years.

Thereafter South Carolina earth was exported extensively to fill the needs of potteries here and abroad, but nearly a century elapsed before it was used again locally. In 1856 William H. Farrar, who had been active in the Bennington Pottery, established the Southern Porcelain Manufacturing Company to exploit the clay banks at Kaolin, South Carolina. The company struggled on for

over twenty years, making a limited amount of porcelain but substantial quantities of ironstone, most of it in
rough pitcher-and-bowl sets and the like.

In the meantime other white clay banks had been discovered in North Carolina. In 1767 Thomas Griffiths, on
commission from Josiah Wedgwood, the English manufacturer, visited the state and brought back some five
tons of potter's earth from a source near Franklin.

Some few years later a supervisory employee from the
ill-fated Bartlam kiln at Charlestown chanced to visit the
Moravian settlement at Salem, North Carolina. There he
provided the potter Gottfried Aust and his apprentice
Rudolph Christ with instructions for the preparation of
Queensware. Then in 1773, William Ellis, last of the
Bartlam employees, spent some time at the settlement
providing further advice on the making of white earthenware.

The Moravians undertook the task of manufacturing
what they described as "English Queensware and Tor-
toise-Shell, that is, a fine pottery resembling porcelain;
the former is lighter than straw color, and the latter is
mottled, like a Tortoise Shell." References to "fine pottery" and "washed" (*i.e.*, refined) clay make it clear that
Queensware was made at Salem at least until 1786. The
congregation records also indicate that this pottery was
mold-made, and, in fact, portions of molds used to add
embossed decoration to the vessels have been found in
the course of excavation at the old community. One of
these forms is marked R C, indicating that the owner was
Rudolph Christ.

The Salem excavations, which are continuing, promise
to throw substantial light on the techniques and products

of pre-1800 potters. A substantial amount of what has been unearthed is now on display at the Old Salem restoration in Winston-Salem, North Carolina.

Maryland and West Virginia

Minor shops in other Southern states notwithstanding, the chief source of whiteware sold in the area was Baltimore, Maryland. Here Edwin Bennett was listing his establishment as a "China Ware Factory" in 1846, at which time he was manufacturing cream-colored or C.C. ware. By the 1860s his Central Avenue pottery had added a line of ironstone tableware.

The famous rendition of Pickett's Charge, high point for the Confederate forces and focus of much emotion, North and South, during the 1870s, was transfer printed at the Bennett works around 1870. The body was cream colored and the design, a central panorama surrounded by floral borders, was typical of current English pieces. The platter, illustrated on page 142d, may be seen at the Maryland Historical Society.

Between 1850 and 1900 the Bennett plant turned out a large number of whiteware and ironstone vessels, and much of this is still available to collectors.

There was substantial local competition. D. F. Haynes' Chesapeake Pottery was established in 1879, and it produced whitewares, including Majolica, until at least 1908. Other kilns were the Monumental Pottery Company, which was founded by Bullock and Miller in 1881 to make a line of cream-colored and graniteware; Hammill, Brown and Company's Maryland Queensware Factory, which specialized in the same wares from 1879 until the late 1880s; and the Maryland Pottery Company (*c.* 1879–1905), a maker of semi-porcelain or hotel china. All these firms marked their output.

West Virginia has been for many years a major manufacturing center for common tableware. Wheeling is the traditional center, and in 1879 the Wheeling Pottery Company made the state's first whiteware. Ironstone marked THE WHEELING/STONE-CHINA/POTTERY CO. is well known. Several other plants graced the city: the La Belle Pottery (absorbed by Wheeling Pottery Company in 1889); the West Virginia China Company, a maker of ironstone between 1890 and 1895; and its successor, the Ohio Valley China Company, active until after the turn of the century.

At New Cumberland was the Chelsea China Company, which turned out a substantial amount of white earthenware between 1888 and 1893. Ironstone from this manufactory was impressed with a star and crescent moon and the phrase CHELSEA WHITE GRANITE.

Directly across the Ohio River from East Liverpool is Newell, West Virginia, from 1854 until the 1950s home of the Edwin M. Knowles China Company. White earthenware was first manufactured here in 1872, and for many years Knowles was one of the nation's leading tableware producers. The Homer Laughlin China Company at the same town has produced ironstone since the 1870s. Its marks, LAUGHLIN/WHITE GRANITE, HOMER LAUGHLIN/HOTEL/CHINA and PREMIUM STONE CHINA/HOMER LAUGHLIN, grace a wide variety of ware from ashtrays to pitchers.

Perhaps 50 per cent of all ironstone china found in antique shops bears the stamp of one or the other of these

IV / Whitewares

Newell firms. Much of it is late, dating to the 1920s and 1930s. Since, however, little available American whiteware was made prior to 1870, antiquity becomes a relative matter here.

3

Midwestern Whitewares

Ohio

The ironstone platter illustrated on page 142f bears the mark of Knowles, Taylor and Knowles, one of the best known of East Liverpool's many whiteware manufacturers. Isaac Knowles began to make yellow clay products here in 1854 as a partner of Isaac Harvey. By 1859 their advertisements in the *Ohio State Directory & Gazeteer* made reference to a line of "variegated enameled Queensware," and once the firm became Knowles, Taylor and Knowles in 1870, the mass production of ironstone and other whitewares was instituted. The mark KT & K appears on great quantities of tableware made between 1872 and 1900, much of it, like this piece, undecorated and relatively crude.

Queensware was made in several other early Liverpool plants including Croxall and Cartright (1856–98) and Foster and Garner (1857–63).

Ironstone, however, was the major pre-1900 product, with a large number of potteries converting to this specialty in the 1870s. One of these was the Vodrey Pottery Company, better known as Vodrey and Brother, which introduced graniteware in 1879. This durable ceramic was still being manufactured in 1925, at which time the Vodrey firm had grown to encompass thirty kilns and over three thousand employees. This factory has employed several whiteware marks, including HOTEL/V.P. CO., VODREY & BRO./STONE CHINA and HOTEL/VB in a wreath.

Many other East Liverpool shops made whitewares from creamware to white earthenware. Some of those whose marked pieces are most common are George S. Harker and Company (1851–90), S. & W. Baggott (1853–95), Henry Brunt and Son (1856–95), and Goodwin, Fleutke and Company (1857–79). Most of these companies or their predecessors also produced C.C. Ware, Rockingham, and similar lines before or simultaneously with graniteware and the earthenwares.

Ohio had many other white clay centers. At Crooksville Lazalier, Burley and Company ran the Crooksville Pottery from 1846 until 1890. Among the popular later wares was hotel china transfer decorated with flower patterns and marked CROOKSVILLE C. CO. The Carrollton China Company (the term "china company" was often used though a plant might produce only whitewares, not porcelain) of Salineville is another of the later firms whose table settings appear often in second-hand shops and antique stores. It was founded in 1901. Of not much earlier vintage was the Salem China Company, operating in Salem from 1895 until at least 1926. Both establishments offered a full line of ironstone and white earthenware. Other latecomers were the Ohio China Company of East Palestine (1896) and the Wellsville Pottery Company, managed by Morley and Company for the production of Majolica and semi-porcelain from 1879 well into the twentieth century.

Illinois, Indiana, and Missouri

The earliest Illinois whitewares were made at Peoria, where Christopher Fenton and Decius Clark, both of whom had previously been active at Bennington, Vermont, manufactured some creamware between 1859 and 1862. Their successor, The American Pottery Company, is said to have continued this specialty until 1873. In the early 1870s the Peoria manufactory was taken over by Joseph Jager, who, after making stoneware for a few years, began the production of ironstone, which was sold until the kiln shut down some time after 1900. Jager's tableware was initially marked with several variations of the British crest. He later adopted the initials P.P. CO. in an entwined pattern as well as the impression HOTEL P.P. CO. with an arrow.

Indiana also had a major whiteware center, Evansville, where at least two different factories existed. In 1884 August and Lewis Uhl, whose Evansville Pottery had made stoneware since the 1860s, entered into a new partnership, Benninghof, Uhl and Company. The firm began to manufacture ironstone and white earthenware, both of which were continued after reorganization in 1891 as the Crown Pottery. The latter corporation frequently and appropriately stamped its wares with some variation of a crown.

The second Evansville factory had a rather brief life. It was established in 1882 by A. M. Beck for the manu-

facture of Majolica but lasted no more than three years.
I know of no existent pottery traceable to this plant.

At Troy, Indiana, the yellow ware firms of Benjamin
Hincho and Saunders and Wilson also made cream-
colored ware from 1850 until the middle 1880s.

Missouri potters made several attempts at finer earthenware, all unsuccessful. Giles F. Filley of Breman, a St.
Louis suburb, advertised Queensware in 1844, and four
years later Frederick Woolford, who had been in the
stoneware business at Caledonia since 1840, entered the
same field.

Woolford worked alone from 1848 until 1852, when
he entered into a partnership with Elihu Shepard. They
built a shop at Kaolin, Missouri, where, as the name sug-
gests, there were rich deposits of white clay, and hired
twenty-one English potters to make Queensware. The
business lost more money each year until it was shut
down in 1858.

Only one other attempt was made, this by James Post,
the Cape Girardeau yellow ware potter who is known
to have manufactured C.C. ware in the early 1880s.

4

Potters of the West

Clay suitable for the making of fine earthenware was not common beyond the Mississippi, nor, until the twentieth century, did the population justify such an industry. The few manufactories which did develop were confined to California and Colorado.

Colorado

The rich clay banks at Golden were utilized for simple white earthen dinnerware by the Geijsbeek Pottery Company, established there in 1899. This plant was still in operation as late as 1910, but I know of no pieces traceable to its kilns. A similar manufactory, the Denver China and Pottery Company, opened in that city in 1904. Utilitarian whitewares were also made here for some years.

California

Southern California was the site of several whiteware factories. Shown on page 142c is a sponge-decorated white earthenware bowl from the Elsinore Pottery Company at Elsinore. This piece is representative of a ware type widely collected today. Spongeware, as it is known, is made by applying color (usually blue or green) to a white clay base, then bathing the vessel in clear alkaline glaze. Since the decorative hue was often put on with a color-soaked sponge, the term spongeware became common. The type is most commonly found in the form of bowls and pitchers. As only a few such pieces are marked, it is difficult to distinguish the domestic product from similar English ware.

The Elsinore Pottery Works was established in the late 1880s or early 1890s to take advantage of local deposits of potter's earth described as the best in the state. The business came to an end around 1935, and the mixing bowl illustrated probably dates from sometime after the turn of the century. It is marked ELSINORE POTTERY CO./ ELSINORE, CALIFORNIA.

J. A. Bauer and Company of Los Angeles is also known to have made whiteware, again in the form of serving and mixing bowls. Quite a bit of this crockery may still be found in California.

Yellow ware: mixing bowl, Roseville Pottery Co., Roseville, Ohio, c. 1900; jelly mold, New England, c. 1890; covered bowl, Ohio, c. 1890; Rockingham custard cup, Ohio, c. 1910. *(Private Collection.)*

Ohio and New Jersey yellow ware mixing bowls, pie plates, and storage crock, c. 1870–1900. *(Private Collection.)*

Stoneware preserve jar, John B. Ziegler, Bellevue, Nebraska, c. 1865. *(Courtesy of Nebraska State Historical Society.)*

Rockingham ware pitchers, Bennett Pottery, Baltimore, c. 1885. *(Courtesy of Maryland Historical Society.)*

Yellow ware preserve jar, Trule Stevens, Nemaha, Nebraska, 1860. *(Courtesy of Nebraska State Historical Society.)*

Blue sponge-decorated white earthenware bowl, Elsinore Pottery, California, c. 1900; glazed yellow ware bowl, Bauer Pottery, Los Angeles, California, c. 1910; glazed yellow ware custard cup, Pacific Pottery, Elsinore, California, c. 1900. *(Courtesy of Margaret Key.)*

Transfer-decorated white earthenware platter, Bennett Pottery, Baltimore, Maryland, c. 1870. (*Courtesy of Maryland Historical Society.*)

Ironstone mixing bowl, Anchor Pottery, Trenton, New Jersey, c. 1895; pie plate, New Jersey, c. 1900; mortar and pestle, Carr China Co., Grafton, West Virginia, c. 1910. (*Private Collection.*)

Transfer-decorated ironstone pitcher, cup and saucer, Onondaga Pottery Co., Syracuse, New York, 1876. (*Courtesy of Syracuse China Corporation.*)

Ironstone pitcher, Chester Pottery Co., Phoenixville, Pennsylvania, c. 1895; platter, Knowles, Taylor & Knowles, East Liverpool, Ohio, c. 1875; egg cup, Chenango China Co., New Castle, Pennsylvania, c. 1901. *(Private Collection.)*

Porcelain teapot, Coors Porcelain Co., Coors, Colorado, c. 1910–14. *(Courtesy of State Historical Society of Colorado.)*

Lotus ware porcelain vase, Knowles, Taylor & Knowles, East Liverpool, Ohio, c. 1888–98. *(Courtesy of the Brooklyn Museum, gift of Arthur W. Clement.)*

Belleek porcelain vase, Ott & Brewer, Trenton, New Jersey, c. 1883–
92. *(Courtesy of the Brooklyn Museum, gift of Mrs. Willard C.
Brinton.)*

V

Porcelain

PORCELAIN, or china, as it is more commonly called, occupies an ambiguous role in ceramic collecting. The remarkably delicate effects which can be achieved in chinaware coupled with the excitement of the unknown (the manufacturing process, though understood in eighth-century Chinese shops, was not developed in Europe until the eighteenth century) led to an early interest in its preservation. As a consequence a substantial number of pieces from American manufactories have been preserved.

The factories, however, were almost entirely in the East and in Ohio. As a result the field has little local interest outside these areas. In most sections of the country collectors cannot seek locally made pre-1900 porcelain. There simply isn't any.

TECHNIQUES *of* MANUFACTURE

The relative scarcity of antique American porcelain is directly related to the ware, which differs greatly from other ceramics in being composed not of a clay or several clays but of an artificial mixture generally containing, in the case of hard porcelain, kaolin (a claylike aluminum silicate), ground flint, and feldspar. Baked at an extremely high temperature, this blend becomes steel hard, vitreous, non-absorbent, and translucent. If unglazed it is spoken of as parian ware, a medium used at Bennington and Brooklyn to imitate marble in cast statues and ornaments.

A second type, soft-paste porcelain, was essentially a substitute for the former. Here powdered glass was added to the batch to secure vitrification at lower temperatures. It was later learned that phosphate (bone ash) would accomplish a similar result, the ware being known, understandably, as bone china. It is some what softer than hard china and slightly absorbent.

All porcelain was baked in a double oven, the first stage or firing taking place in the cooler upper level, where the ware was brought to the biscuit stage. When removed, it was brittle enough to be broken in the fingers and still porous. The biscuit or bisque was then dipped in a tub of glaze consisting of its own body ingredients in different proportions, those which fuse first now predominating. The porous vessel absorbed the liquid in the glaze, leaving a fine, dry mineral coat on its surface. The pieces were then placed in separate saggers (unglazed clay boxes used to protect baking ware) and fired in the main oven at maximum temperature. The glaze of softer composition melted into the body; the whole was then vitrified into a homogeneous glasslike form.

Porcelain was never easy to make (the Chinese had monopolized the field for hundreds of years) and always expensive. Materials had often to be bought from a great distance. Special ovens and the services of particularly skilled artisans added to overhead. Consequently, the ware has been produced at relatively few centers. The earliest shops in Philadelphia and New York have left some examples, all of which are in museums or private collections. Later ware is available, but often at a premium, as porcelain has long been one of the most sought-after ceramics.

I

Eastern Chinaware

As the area earliest and most affected by European taste, the East was, understandably, the site of the primal attempts at porcelain making. It was, likewise, the location in which the first successful manufactories were located.

Pennsylvania and New Jersey

Two of the earliest American porcelain factories were located in Philadelphia. In 1769 Gousse Bonnin and George Morris began the business there. Though their shop lasted only until 1772, several authenticated examples of Bonnin and Morris porcelain remain, one of which was found at a bazaar and purchased for a few cents!

A half-century later, in the same city, William Tucker established the first successful manufactory in this line. He began to make tableware, vases, and the like in 1826, taking Thomas Hulme as a partner in 1828 and Alexander Hemphill some three years later. Examples are known from all three periods. At Tucker's death in 1832 control of the firm passed to the partner's wealthy father, Joseph Hemphill, who operated it until 1838.

Quite a few pieces from the Tucker shop have survived. They are primarily pitchers, jardinières, plates, and vases with a strong classical motif. Representative examples may be seen at the Metropolitan Museum and the Brooklyn Museum in New York, and the Henry Ford Museum in Dearborn, Michigan.

Other Philadelphia china makers were Abraham Miller, who exhibited porcelain at the city's Franklin Institute as early as 1824; Smith, Fife and Company, c. 1830; Abraham Bechtel, active in the 1850s; and C. Fries, a china maker of the 1860s. Richard C. Remmey, whose stoneware monogrammed RCR is highly prized, also made porcelain, continuing into the 1890s. There are only a few existent vessels attributable to these craftsmen.

In New Jersey, the Jersey City Porcelain and Earthenware Company was active from 1825 until 1828, and it was the first of many such manufactories in the nineteenth century.

By mid-century Trenton had several plants, the foremost of which was William Young and Company, established in 1853. Young and his sons had a shop on the Raritan Canal that made a variety of chinaware until 1879. In that year the firm was reorganized as the Willetts Manufacturing Company, under which name it continued into the twentieth century. Porcelain from this factory is well known. Examples, primarily vases, pitchers, and dishware, are available for examination at the Newark and New Jersey State Museums as well as the Brooklyn Museum.

Ott and Brewer's well known Eturia Works also made porcelain from at least 1865 until 1892. Illustrated on page 142h is an Ott vase in Beleek porcelain, an extremely delicate and thin bodied variation. Henry Speeler's Assanpink Pottery was active in the same field during the 1860s and 1870s.

Richard Millington and John Astbury built a kiln on Perry Street in Trenton in the 1850s, which passed later into the hands of Thomas Maddock and Company, who continued the business into the 1900s. This plant was making porcelain by 1865, and the line was maintained by later owners.

There were many similar manufactories in the community: the Trenton China Company (1859–91); the East Trenton Porcelain Company, active in the 1870s; Alpaugh and McGowan (*c.* 1880–83); and the International Pottery Company (1879–1900), to mention a few of the better-known works.

While Trenton dominated the trade, Jersey City had a fine-ware kiln, as did Gloucester, where the American Porcelain Manufacturing Company and its successor, the Gloucester Porcelain Company, made ornate china pitchers from 1854 until 1872.

New York

New York did not have a significant early china history such as existed in Pennsylvania and New Jersey. It was after 1840 that two porcelain factories opened in the Greenpoint section of Brooklyn. One was owned by Charles Cartlidge and Company, the other by William Boch and his brothers, Anthony and Victor. The establishment dates of these plants have been given as 1848 and 1853 respectively, but neither year can be correct, since both firms appear in the *Greenpoint & Bushwick Directory* of 1844–45.

In any case, Cartlidge made soft- then hard-paste porcelain until his business failed in 1856. At least some of the former was made from human rather than animal ash. The incident, as reported by Edwin A. Barber in his *Historical Sketch of the Greenpoint Porcelain Works* (1895), is particularly appropriate to the rise of production-line ceramic manufacture:

> In grading some land at Hunters Point, near Green Point, bones of buried Indians were exhumed, and these were utilized in the manufacture of articles on which appropriate and particularly happy inscriptions, prepared by Mr. Cartlidge, were placed!

Thus the factory system which was to feed on and make obsolete the skills of individual craftsmen first utilized as raw material the bones of those upon whose stolen lands the kilns stood.

Following Cartlidge's failure the Boch family prospered until 1862, when they sold out to Thomas C. Smith, who continued the business as the Union Porcelain Works. Both firms are noted for their china pitchers, mugs, vases, and other fancy ware, much of which has survived in museums and private collections. Boch also had a line of door- and furniture knobs and trimmings as well as funerary images, such as lambs and the like, to be mounted on gravestones.

Besides Smith's Union Porcelain Works, which continued into the twentieth century, there were several other china factories in New York City. James L. Jensen managed the Empire China Works from 1873 until well after 1900, and William Boch, Jr., son of the old proprietor, built the French China Manufactory in Corona, Queens, before 1868. He operated it for only two or three years, making tableware and knobs. After his abandoned shop burned in 1879, it was rebuilt as the Corona Porcelain Manufacturing Company. This venture was equally short-lived, closing soon after 1882. In Manhattan James Carr's New York City Pottery manufactured parian porcelain during the 1870s and 1880s.

Outside the metropolitan area porcelain was made at Syracuse, where the still active Onondaga Pottery Company developed a successful variant of hard porcelain in 1888. This ware is still being made. The Chittenango Pottery Company in the community of the same name experimented briefly with bone china after its organization in 1897. Two disastrous fires put an end to this project.

New York porcelain is widely collected, and examples may be purchased, though at substantial prices. Good collections may be seen at the Brooklyn and Metropolitan museums as well as the New York Historical Society.

Vermont and Massachusetts

There were only two nineteenth-century porcelain producers in the New England area. Christopher Webber Fenton brought the English potter John Harrison to Bennington, Vermont, in 1843 to assist in development of a china manufactory. Some parian ware was made that year, and during 1847 and 1848 this porcelain was manufactured on a commercial basis. The Wadsworth Atheneum in Hartford, Connecticut, has several parian pitchers impressed FENTON'S WORKS/BENNINGTON/VERMONT.

Though references are obscure during the next few years, it appears from bills of sale and other evidence that parian continued to be made at Bennington after Fenton established his United States Pottery Company in 1853. The marks U.S.P. and UNITED STATES POTTERY CO./BEN-NINGTON, VT. appear on parian pieces, primarily pitchers. It is also known that folk figures, children and animals, were modeled in this medium. Needless to say, Bennington china is sold at a premium.

Boston's New England Pottery Company advertised parian as early as 1862, and at least one mark is known, the monogram N.E.P. CO., which appears on a porcelain pitcher in the collection of the Bennington Museum. Though this manufactory continued until 1914, it does not seem that china was made in any substantial amount. Certainly, few examples remain.

2

Porcelain in the South

South of Philadelphia china making was never particularly successful, even though some of the very earliest American porcelain may have been made below the Mason-Dixon Line.

South Carolina and Louisiana

In 1739 Andrew Duche of Savannah, Georgia, was recorded in official documents as experimenting with "china." This ware was described as being translucent, and certain blue-decorated porcelain vessels attributed to Duche have turned up. The manufactory failed within a short period of time, and the potter left Georgia.

William H. Farrar's Southern Porcelain Manufacturing Company at Kaolin, South Carolina, was somewhat more fortunate. A limited amount of china tableware was made there in the 1850s and 1860s; and during the Civil War porcelain insulators were manufactured for use on Confederate telegraph lines. One of the guiding figures at Kaolin was Josiah Jones, who had been active in management of the Cartlidge works at Brooklyn.

The Deep South had only one fine-ware manufactory.

In 1881 Hernandez and Saley of New Orleans opened the Louisiana Porcelain Works. They continued until 1890, but little is known of the firm or its products. Considering the relatively recent period of operation, it is reasonable to assume that examples of this plant's porcelain can be uncovered.

3

The West

Porcelain manufacture spread slowly and late to the Western states. The capital and know-how necessary were not available until the last quarter of the nineteenth century, though a few firms had put the ware into production prior to that time.

Ohio

Perhaps first in the field was William Bloor, who introduced parian at East Liverpool in 1859. He did not continue after 1862, and others hesitated to take the same path. However, in 1887 Knowles, Taylor and Knowles of Liverpool imported an Irish potter familiar with the making of belleek, a thin, highly translucent porcelain variant somewhat akin to parian. Two years later he produced the state's first belleek, later developing lotusware, a not significantly different china. An example of the later is shown on page 142g. Substantial numbers of ewers, bonbon dishes, pinholders, and the like were manufactured at Knowles between 1891 and 1898. The mark KTK CO./ LOTUSWARE is well known to Midwestern collectors. Taylor, Smith and Taylor, also in East Liverpool, made comparable tableware after 1900.

It was late in the century before other Ohio communities entered the field. At Franklin the Franklin Porcelain Company proved unprofitable after a brief period of activity, *c.* 1880–84. The Summit China Company of Akron appears to have made some porcelain between 1890 and 1900, and the Oliver China Company of Sebring, established 1899, put out a line of china tableware impressed VERUS/PORCELAIN. There were similar manufactories in other parts of the state, and today Ohio continues to be a major source of American porcelain.

California and Colorado

West of the Mississippi the little fine dishware owned by the pioneers was imported, not locally made. While there is said to have been a china factory in Los Angeles around 1875, I know of nothing attributable thereto. The mountain states had at least one attempt. In 1910 the Coors Porcelain Company at Coors, Colorado, undertook the manufacture of porcelain dinner sets. A teapot from this plant is shown on page 142f. It is a striking example of balance and good taste, something rare in earlier porcelain. Apparently there was little market for such a luxury. In 1914 the company transferred its efforts to sanitary earthenwares.

APPENDIX

A LIST OF EARLY AMERICAN POTTERIES

This appendix is intended to enable collectors to pinpoint pottery manufactories that existed in their areas of interest. It is not intended to be a complete schedule of pre-1900 potters. For more exhaustive lists on New England one should refer to Lura Watkins' *Early New England Potters and Their Wares* (Archon, 1968). The many Ohio and New Jersey kilns are catalogued in John Ramsey's *Early American Pottery and China* (Boston: Hale, Cushman & Flint, 1939), and the New York shops in my own *Early Potters and Potteries of New York State* (New York: Funk & Wagnalls, 1970).

LOCALITY	POTTERY	PERIOD ACTIVE	TYPE OF WARE
	ALABAMA		
Bedford	Peter Cribbs & Wife	c.1865–90	stoneware
Coosada	McLean Pottery Co.	c.1880–1900	stoneware
Franklin County	Franklin County Pottery	c.1897	stoneware
Pegram	J. W. Williams	c.1890	stoneware
Pine Springs	Guthrie & Lloyd	c.1887	stoneware
Rock Mills	F. M. Boyd	c.1887	stoneware
Sterrett	W. H. Falkner	c.1887	stoneware
Tuscaloosa	Daniel Cribbs & Son	c.1829–90	stoneware
	C. K. Oliver	c.1855	stoneware

Appendix

LOCALITY	POTTERY	PERIOD ACTIVE	TYPE OF WARE

ARKANSAS

LOCALITY	POTTERY	PERIOD ACTIVE	TYPE OF WARE
Benton	W. H. Bennett	1890–1900	stoneware
	F. W. Bush	1879–81	stoneware
	Lafayette Glass	c.1868–79	stoneware
	Samuel Henderson	1884–96	stoneware
	E. L. Herrick	1891–97	stoneware
	John F. Hyten	1881–82	stoneware
	Hyten Brothers	1895–1912	stoneware
	Charles & H. A. Rhodenbaugh	1886–1900	stoneware
	Tyler & Sharks	1879–81	stoneware
	A. E. Wilbur	1876–87	stoneware
	Frank Woolsey	1882–95	stoneware
Boonesborough	J. D. Wilbur	c.1884	stoneware
Cane Hill	H. T. Caldwell & Co.	c.1860	redware
	William S. Crawley	c.1846–74	redware
Malvern	O. C. & T. N. Atchison	c.1888–98	stoneware
	E. A. Nunn & Co.	c.1874–92	stoneware
Mansfield	Lafayette Glass	c.1858	stoneware
Murfreesboro	Lafayette Glass	c.1860	stoneware
Paragould	Black & Simmemon	c.1898	stoneware
Princeton	Bird Brothers	c.1843–62	stoneware
	John Welch	1862–74	stoneware
Rector	Garner & Grubbs	c.1898	stoneware
Story	J. S. Robertson	c.1898	stoneware
Texarkana	D. S. Collins & Co.	c.1888–92	stoneware

CALIFORNIA

LOCALITY	POTTERY	PERIOD ACTIVE	TYPE OF WARE
Alameda	Clarke Potteries	c.1900	?
East Oakland	Daniel Brannon (Pioneer Pottery)	1856–c.87	Rockingham, yellow ware
	Henry Bundock	1872–c.84	stoneware
	Miller & Winsor (California Pottery)	1875–c.99	flowerpots
Elsinore	Elsinore Pottery Co.	c.1921–23	whiteware
	Elsinore Pottery & Fire Clay, Co.	1885–1888	earthenware
Lincoln	Gladding, McBean & Co.	1875–	whiteware

LOCALITY	POTTERY	PERIOD ACTIVE	TYPE OF WARE
Los Angeles	J. A. Bauer & Co.	c.1890–1958	stoneware, redware, yellow ware
	Los Angeles Stoneware Co.	1900–1903	stoneware
	Pacific Clay Manufacturing Co.	c.1894–1910	yellow ware
	Gladding, McBean & Co.	c.1875–1945	redware, whiteware
Michigan Bar	J. W. Orr & Co.	1859–96	stoneware
Sacramento	N. Clark & Sons	c.1887	?
	Sacramento Pottery	1855–c.79	stoneware
San Francisco	Steiger Pottery Works	c.1895	?
	Tracy Brothers & Co.	c.1887	?

COLORADO

Coors	Coors Porcelain Co.	1910–14	porcelain
Denver	Denver China & Pottery Co.	c.1904–?	whiteware
	Montague Pottery	1893–?	flowerpots
Golden	Henry Bell (Golden City Pottery)	c.1871	redware
	Geijsbeek Pottery Co.	1899–c.1910	whiteware

CONNECTICUT

Goshen	Hervey Brooks	c.1803–64	redware
Greenwich	Adam Staats	c.1750–69	stoneware
	Abraham Mead	c.1769–91	stoneware
Hartford	Seth Goodwin & Sons	c.1795–1832	redware, stoneware
	Nathaniel Seymour	c.1790–1842	redware, stoneware
	Daniel Goodale, Jr., & Co.	1818–30	stoneware
	Horace Goodwin & Mack Webster	c.1830–57	stoneware
	Orson Seymour & Co.	c.1857–85	stoneware
Litchfield	John Pierce	c.1752–80	redware

Appendix

LOCALITY	POTTERY	PERIOD ACTIVE	TYPE OF WARE
New Haven	Absalom Stedman	c.1825–31	stoneware
	S. L. Pewtress	c.1868–87	stoneware
Norwich	Armstrong & Wentworth	1814–34	stoneware
	Sidney Risley & Son	c.1845–81	Rockingham, stoneware
	Norwich Pottery Works	1881–95	stoneware
Norwalk	Asa Hoyt	c.1796–1819	redware
	Absalom Day	c.1793–1841	redware, yellow ware
	Noah Day	1841–49	stoneware
	Asa E. Smith & Co.	c.1825–87	redware, stoneware
Quasset	Thomas Bugbee, Jr.	1793–1843	redware
Stonington	Adam Staats, Jr.	c.1778–1826	stoneware
	William Staats & Co.	c.1811–35	stoneware

DELAWARE

LOCALITY	POTTERY	PERIOD ACTIVE	TYPE OF WARE
Hockessin	Abner Marshall	c.1859–66	Rockingham
Wilmington	William Reiss	c.1851	earthenware
	William Hare	c.1857–87	earthenware
	George Zeigler	c.1857	earthenware
	A. Neumayer	c.1887	earthenware

DISTRICT OF COLUMBIA

POTTERY	PERIOD ACTIVE	TYPE OF WARE
Joseph Straub	c.1853–68	earthenware
Enoch Burnett	c.1853–69	stoneware
Charles Rhinehart	c.1864–66	redware
Louis Lee	c.1869	redware
John Rhinehart	c.1863	redware

FLORIDA

LOCALITY	POTTERY	PERIOD ACTIVE	TYPE OF WARE
Jacksonville	West End Pottery Co.	c.1910	?
Knox Hill	M. M. Odum & Robert Turnlee	1859–60	stoneware
Lake Butler	H. F. York	c.1880–1900	redware

LOCALITY	POTTERY	PERIOD ACTIVE	TYPE OF WARE
		GEORGIA	
Albany	Lawrence Lovett	_c._1886–87	stoneware
Banning	S. A. Hornsby	_c._1883–87	stoneware
Bolton	Brown Pottery	_c._1890–1900	stoneware
Bogart	J. D. Brewer	_c._1870–1900	stoneware
Bowenville	C. C. Hornsley	_c._1881–82	stoneware
Byram	James Long & Family	_c._1820–1900	stoneware
Cartersville	Gordy Pottery	_c._1865–1900	stoneware
Cleveland	Meader Pottery	_c._1830–1900	stoneware
Cross Keys	A. T. Davidson & Bro.	_c._1881–87	stoneware
Galliardes	Thomas Dickson	_c._1870–1900	stoneware
	H. N. Long	_c._1880–1900	stoneware
	H. D. Marshall	_c._1880–1900	stoneware
Gillsville	Hewell Pottery	_c._1830–1900	stoneware
	J. C. Holcomb	_c._1830–87	stoneware
	Colbert Pottery	_c._1870–1900	stoneware
Leo	Meader Pottery	_c._1890–1900	stoneware
	Dorsey, Enos & Tarplin	_c._1880–82	stoneware
	I. Cravens	_c._1883–84	stoneware
Lizella	Middle Georgia Pottery	_c._1870–1900	stoneware
Meansville	Rogers Pottery	_c._1850–1900	stoneware
	Bishop Pottery	_c._1850–1900	stoneware
Milledgeville	J. W. McMillan	_c._1867–1900	stoneware
Mossy Creek	J. H. Craven & Son	_c._1883–87	stoneware
	J. S. & L. S. Brownlow	_c._1883–87	stoneware
Savannah	Andrew Duche	_c._1738–43	redware
Stevens Pottery Post Office	Henry Stevens	_c._1815–65	stoneware
	W. C. & I. H. Stevens & Co.	_c._1865–1900	stoneware
Thomasville	Rogers Pottery Co.	_c._1830–1900	stoneware
Warthen	John Redfern	_c._1883–87	stoneware

Appendix

LOCALITY	POTTERY	PERIOD ACTIVE	TYPE OF WARE
	ILLINOIS		
Anna	C. & W. Kirkpatrick (Anna Pottery)	1859–*c.*90	stoneware
Chicago	John S. Classen	*c.*1860	?
Galena	Alfred Sackett & John Wagden	*c.*1858–69	redware, stoneware
	Andrew Jennings	*c.*1880–87	stoneware
Livingston	Abel English	*c.*1868	?
	O. L. Wilson	*c.*1868	?
Macomb	Macomb Pottery Co.	*c.*1880–1906	stoneware
	Eagle Pottery Co.	*c.*1883–1900	stoneware
Monmouth	Western Stoneware Co.	*c.*1870–90	stoneware
	Monmouth Pottery Co.	*c.*1890–1905	stoneware
Mound City	Cornwall Kirkpatrick	1857–59	?
Peoria	Christopher Fenton & Decius Clark	1859–62	yellow ware, whiteware
	A. M. Johnson (American Pottery)	1864–73	yellow ware
	Peoria Pottery (Joseph Jager)	*c.*1864–89	stoneware, whiteware
Quincy	Charles Brenner	*c.*1866–70	?
Ripley	John M. Ebey	*c.*1836	stoneware
	John N. Stout	*c.*1866–87	stoneware, Rockingham
Vermilionville	John Kirkpatrick	*c.*1837–64	?
White Hall	Michael Baker	*c.*1830	stoneware
	Hill, Prindle & Co.	*c.*1887	?
	INDIANA		
Annapolis	H. S. Atcheson	1841–1906	stoneware
	Welch & Lee	*c.*1887	stoneware
Brazil	Isaac Cordrey	*c.*1868–69	yellow ware
	Tourpert & Becker	*c.*1859–90	yellow ware

164

LOCALITY	POTTERY	PERIOD ACTIVE	TYPE OF WARE
Clay City	B. Griffith	c.1846–1908	?
Evansville	A. & L. Uhl	c.1864–87	stoneware
	Benninghof, Uhl & Co.	1884–91	whiteware
	Crown Pottery Co.	c.1891–1905	whiteware
	L. Daum & Sons	c.1864–66	stoneware
	A. M. Beck	c.1882–84	Majolica, stoneware
Fountain City	Robert D. Bailey	1853–60	?
Fort Wayne	Samuel Lillie	c.1866	?
Hartford City	Cline & Son	c.1866	?
Indianapolis	John F. W. Myer	c.1866	earthenware
Logotee	Logotee Pottery	c.1842–92	stoneware
New Albany	William Keller	c.1865	stoneware
Richmond	Bott, Hamersley & Co.	c.1875	yellow ware
Shoals	Devol & Catterson	c.1870	stoneware
	William James	c.1887	stoneware
Troy	James Clews	1834–39	yellow ware
	Jabez Vodrey	1839–46	Rockingham, yellow ware
	Saunders & Wilson	c.1851–63	whiteware, yellow ware
	Ben Hincho	c.1865–85	whiteware, yellow ware

IOWA

LOCALITY	POTTERY	PERIOD ACTIVE	TYPE OF WARE
Attica	Joseph F. Jennings	c.1875	stoneware
	Ira Kendrick	c.1875	stoneware
Boonesborough	C. C. Hinshaw	c.1865	?
	M. A. Griffee	c.1888	?
Burlington	Turley Brothers	c.1870–90	?
Carlisle	Matthew Farley	c.1887	?
	McBurney & Franklin	c.1887	?
Cedar Rapids	Francisco Smith	c.1865	?

Appendix

LOCALITY	POTTERY	PERIOD ACTIVE	TYPE OF WARE
Coalport	William Welch	1847–*c*.60	stoneware
	Thomas H. Smith & Son	*c*.1860–80	stoneware
Davenport	Davenport Pottery	*c*.1885–87	stoneware
Des Moines	E. L. & J. L. Weeks	*c*.1887	?
Eldora	Henry Tolman & Co.	*c*.1865	?
	H. C. Sweet	*c*.1887	?
Fort Dodge	Fort Dodge Pottery Co.	*c*.1885	stoneware
	Union Pottery Works	*c*.1887	stoneware
Iowa City	Ohnhause & Baker	*c*.1865	stoneware
Knoxville	Silas & John King	*c*.1880–1909	?
Lowell	Edward Melcher	*c*.1870	stoneware
	Lowell Pottery	*c*.1880–90	stoneware
Ottumwa	John P. Williams	*c*.1865	?
Parrish	Dennis Melcher & Bro.	*c*.1848–65	stoneware
Red Oak	W. H. Close	*c*.1887	?
Vernon	Robert M. Dickson	*c*.1865–87	?

KANSAS

LOCALITY	POTTERY	PERIOD ACTIVE	TYPE OF WARE
Blooming Grove	I. B. Seigler	*c*.1867–68	?
Clyde	Truellis Stephens	1869–73	stoneware
	Jacob Sohlinger	*c*.1873–82	stoneware
Eudora	Gottlieb Epple	*c*.1860–68	?
Larned	Larned Pottery Co.	*c*.1887	earthenware
Lawrence	Schilling Pottery Works	*c*.1880	redware
	Anton Grutz	*c*.1868	redware
Leavenworth	Julius Keller & Co.	*c*.1860–63	stoneware, earthenware
	John Singer	*c*.1863	?

LOCALITY	POTTERY	PERIOD ACTIVE	TYPE OF WARE
		KENTUCKY	
Bell City	W. B. Howard & Son	*c*.1870–90	stoneware
	W. D. Russell (Bell City Pottery)	*c*.1890–1922	brownware, stoneware
Bybee	Cornelison Pottery	*c*.1809–	stoneware
Covington	Cornwall Kirkpatrick	1839–48	redware
	Eel Herman & Henry Holm	*c*.1859	?
Eddyville	W. P. Bonner	*c*.1856–59	stoneware
Jeffersonville	George Unser	*c*.1865–69	stoneware
Lexington	John Carty & Co.	*c*.1796–1845	redware
Louisville	Lewis Pottery Co.	*c*.1829–36	yellow ware, whiteware
	John & Fred Hancock	*c*.1840	stoneware
	Anton Sauer	*c*.1865–69	stoneware
	George W. Doane	*c*.1838–48	?
	Henry Melcher (Louisville Pottery)	1845–*c*.1922	stoneware
	John Bauer & Co.	*c*.1887–1905	stoneware
	William Frost & Co.	*c*.1836–46	?
	Abraham Dover	*c*.1843–48	redware
Lynville	J. W. Pittman	*c*.1870–1900	brownware
Paducah	A. J. Bauer (Paducah Pottery)	*c*.1886–1900	redware
Pottertown	Falwell & Son	*c*.1920–22	stoneware
Waco	D. Zittel & Co.	*c*.1870–1905	stoneware
	Grimstead & Stone	*c*.1919–22	stoneware
Water Valley	Water Valley Pottery Co.	*c*.1870–90	brownware
Wickcliffe	August Keppner	*c*.1880–1900	brownware
		LOUISIANA	
Jefferson City	William Virgin	*c*.1867–69	?
New Orleans	Hernandez & Saley (Louisiana Porcelain Works)	1881–90	porcelain
	James L. Swan	*c*.1869	?

Appendix

LOCALITY	POTTERY	PERIOD ACTIVE	TYPE OF WARE
	MAINE		
Bangor	Bangor Stoneware Works	*c.*1890–1916	stoneware
Bloomfield	Joseph Philbrick	*c.*1825–70	redware
Buxton	James & Ebenezer Wentworth	*c.*1825–80	redware
Gardiner	Lyman & Clark	*c.*1837–41	stoneware
	Francis A. Plaisted	*c.*1850–74	stoneware
	Gardiner Stoneware Co.	*c.*1874–87	stoneware
Hebron	David Webber & Sons	*c.*1811–85	redware
North Bridgton	Richard F. Kitson	1815–*c.*70	redware
Orrington	George Brooks	*c.*1845–85	redware
Portland	Caleb Crafts & Co.	*c.*1835–41	stoneware
	Portland Stoneware Co.	1850–	stoneware
	Benjamin Dodge & Son	1801–76	redware
	Rufus Lamson & Eben Swasey	1876–82	redware
	Portland Pottery Works	1882–90	redware
Woolrich	John Corliss	1820–*c.*80	redware
Yarmouth	Ebenezer Corliss & George Bruce	1806–50	redware
	David Cleaves & Son	1850–85	redware
	Nathaniel Foster & Sons	1840–90	redware
	Joel Brooks	*c.*1850–80	redware
	MARYLAND		
Bacon Hill	Grosh Pottery	*c.*1880–1900	redware
Baltimore	Peter Perine, Jr.	*c.*1793–1819	redware, stoneware
	Mauldine Perine & Co.	1827–1938	stoneware, redware
	William Linton	*c.*1845–67	stoneware

LOCALITY	POTTERY	PERIOD ACTIVE	TYPE OF WARE
	Edwin Bennett & Co.	c.1846–1938	Rockingham, yellow ware, whiteware
	Maryland Potteries (David, Margaret & James Parr)	c.1815–55	stoneware, redware
	James E. Jones & Co.	c.1834–45	stoneware, redware
	Maryland Queensware Factory	c.1879–83	whiteware
	Monumental Pottery Co.	1881–c.83	whiteware
	Maryland Pottery Co.	1879–c.1905	whiteware
	Peter Herman	1850–72	stoneware
	H. S. Taylor (Jackson Square Pottery)	1872–c.83	stoneware, redware
	D. F. Haynes & Co. (Chesapeake Pottery)	c.1879–1910	porcelain, Majolica, whiteware
Cumberland	Jacob Easter	c.1850	redware, brownware
Fells Point	Henry Remmey	1813–35	?
Hagerstown	Peter Bell, Jr., & Co.	1800–24	redware
	John Bell	c.1820–24	redware
	Henry Weise	c.1870	redware, stoneware
	Martin Happel	c.1890	redware
Rock Springs	Henry Scholfield	1861–95	redware
St. Marys	J. W. Baecher	1853–80	redware
	Adam Kern	1880–92	redware
Taneytown	Samuel Crouse	c.1850	redware
Thurmont	Jacob Lynn	c.1853–80	redware
	Anthony W. Baecher	c.1868–80	redware

Appendix

LOCALITY	POTTERY	PERIOD ACTIVE	TYPE OF WARE

MASSACHUSETTS

LOCALITY	POTTERY	PERIOD ACTIVE	TYPE OF WARE
Berkley	Paul Osborn & Edward Shove	c.1740–60	redware
	William Boyce & Family	c.1765–1876	redware
Beverly	Charles Lawrence	1866–1906	redware
Boston	Jonathan Fenton	1794–96	stoneware
	Edmands & Co.	c.1812–1905	stoneware
	Alexander F. Scott & Co.	c.1870–95	stoneware
	Boston Pottery Co.	1878–1900	stoneware, yellow ware, Rockingham
	Boston Earthenware Manufacturing Co.	c.1852–58	whiteware, yellow ware, Rockingham, porcelain
Cambridge	A. H. Hews & Co.	c.1871–1949	redware
Charlestown	John Runey & Sons	1788–c.1856	redware
	Thomas Symmes & Co.	1743–46	redware, stoneware
Chelsea	Loammi Kendall	1836–c.70	stoneware
Danvers	Osborn Potteries	c.1738–1853	redware
Dorchester	Dorchester Pottery Works	c.1880–	stoneware
East Brookfield	Richard Linley & Abner Wright	1879–88	redware
	James Smith & Co.	c.1868–79	redware
Lynn	William Jackson	1811–15	redware
Merrimacport	William Pecker	c.1784–1820	redware
	James Chase	c.1815–49	redware
	Phineas Chase	1849–63	redware
Northampton	Jonathan Hall	c.1779–1800	redware
Rockport	Lewis Mason	c.1879–85	redware

LOCALITY	POTTERY	PERIOD ACTIVE	TYPE OF WARE
Somerset	Clark Purinton & Sons	c.1750–1835	redware
	Asa Chase & Family	c.1768–1836	redware
	Somerset Pottery	1836–1909	stoneware, redware
	Patrick & William Synan	1893–c.1913	stoneware
South Ashfield	Walter Orcutt & Co.	1848–50	stoneware
	Hastings & Belding	1850–56	stoneware
Taunton	Alex Standish & Franklin Wright	c.1846–55	stoneware
	Franklin T. Wright & Co.	1855–68	stoneware
Weston	Abraham Hews & Family	1765–1871	redware
West Sterling	Wachusett Pottery	1820–87	redware
Whately	Stephen Orcutt & Co.	c.1797–1830	stoneware, redware
	Thomas Crafts & Family	c.1806–61	stoneware, redware
Worcester	Frank Norton & Frederick Hancock	1858–85	stoneware

MICHIGAN

LOCALITY	POTTERY	PERIOD ACTIVE	TYPE OF WARE
Corunna	John Neuffer	c.1863–64	redware
Detroit	Martin Autretsch	c.1863–69	redware
	Theodore Blasley	c.1865	redware
Grand Rapids	David Stiven & Samuel Davis	c.1859–67	?
Hadley	Mortimer Price	c.1863–64	?
Hanover	Elijah Nichols	c.1863–65	?
Ionia	Sage & Dethrick	c.1898–1903	earthenware
Marshall	Aaron Norris	c.1862–64	redware

Appendix

LOCALITY	POTTERY	PERIOD ACTIVE	TYPE OF WARE

MINNESOTA

LOCALITY	POTTERY	PERIOD ACTIVE	TYPE OF WARE
Elmwood	Charles Rees	c.1869–70	redware
Mankato	Henry Kauffer & Theodore Fittler	c.1860–78	stoneware
	Andrew Gapter	c.1875	stoneware
	John A. Sanborn & Co.	c.1880–84	stoneware
Minneapolis	Louis Kampff	1857–76	redware
	Jonas G. Swahn & Sons	1876–1904	redware
	John C. Malchow	c.1870–80	redware
	Julius Gobeaux	c.1895–1901	redware
New Ulm	Dauffenbach, Steckert & Friedman	c.1870	stoneware
Owatonna	Charles C. Cornell	1863–71	stoneware, redware
Redwing	Joseph Pohl	c.1861	redware
	William Philleo & Philander Sprague	1868–77	redware
	David Hallem & Henry Mitchell	c.1877	stoneware
	Red Wing Stoneware Co. (Redwing Pottery)	1877–1967	stoneware, yellow ware
	Minnesota Stoneware Co.	1883–1906	stoneware
	North Star Stoneware Co.	1892–1897	stoneware

MISSOURI

LOCALITY	POTTERY	PERIOD ACTIVE	TYPE OF WARE
Arrow Rock	Caldwell & McCumber	c.1855–60	stoneware
Booneville	F. X. & August Blank	c.1880–90	stoneware
	John M. Jegglin	1868–c.90	stoneware
	George & Nicholas Volrath	c.1860–70	stoneware
	Marcus Williams	1834, 1839–49	stoneware
	Marcus Williams, Jr.	1849–c.60	earthenware
	Charles Weyrich	1870–77	stoneware
Caledonia	Frederick Woolford	1840–c.52	stoneware

LOCALITY	POTTERY	PERIOD ACTIVE	TYPE OF
Calhoun	Calhoun Pottery	1871–c.91	stoneware
	Darby & Sons	1878–89	stoneware
	G. A. Jegglin	1880–93	stoneware
	J. T. Dawson & Son	c.1876	stoneware
	H. J. Underwood & Son	1880–91	stoneware
California	August Blank	1890–c.1900	stoneware
Cape Girardeau	James Post	c.1881–85	Rockingham, whiteware
Clinton	Clinton Pottery Co.	c.1886–91	?
Dexter	Evans Family	c.1850–1942	stoneware
Florence	John M. Hummel	c.1860–90	stoneware
Herman	George M. Sohns	1847–67	redware
Kansas City	Kansas City Pottery	1888–91	stoneware
Kaolin	Frederick Woolford & Elihu Shepard	1852–c.58	whiteware
Lamar	N. F. Fancher	c.1888–91	stoneware
Rocheport	John Cranson	1844–60	stoneware
	W. H. Williamson & Son	1860–82	stoneware
St. Charles	Joseph Oser	1846–1906	redware
St. Joseph	William Bloomfield & Charles McChesney	1867–c.75	stoneware
	C. E. Kemp	c.1867–68	stoneware
St. Louis	John Taylor & John Bradbury	c.1820–21	redware
	Jacob Broun & Co.	c.1860–69	stoneware
	Michael Roth	c.1860–67	stoneware
	Joseph Hirn & Co.	c.1860–69	stoneware
	George Heffner	c.1860	stoneware
	Giles F. Filley	c.1844	whiteware

MISSISSIPPI

Biloxi	—— Mayer	c.1856–90	redware
	Joseph Mayer	1890–1900	redware
	George Ohr	c.1908–10	stoneware

173

Appendix

LOCALITY	POTTERY	PERIOD ACTIVE	TYPE OF WARE

MONTANA

Helena	Jack Busack (Deer Lodge Pottery)	1871–*c*.75	redware

NEBRASKA

Alma	L. E. Guyer (Alma Pottery Works)	1882–83	?
Aurora	J. M. Brown	*c*.1886–87	?
Dakota City	John B. Ziegler & Charles Eckhart	*c*.1859–61, 67	stoneware
	P. Neff	*c*.1866	stoneware
Franklin	F. Sutton	*c*.1886–87	?
Lincoln	Henry Kessler	*c*.1884–85	?
	W. & O. V. Eaton (Lincoln Pottery)	1880–*c*.1903	redware, stoneware
Louisville	J. T. A. Hoover (Louisville Stoneware Manufacturing Co.)	1879–83	stoneware
	Louisville Pottery Works	1884–85	stoneware
	Western Pottery Co.	1886–94	stoneware
	William Wade	*c*.1890–91	?
Nebraska City	The Nebraska City Pottery	*c*.1867	redware
Nemaha	Trule Stevens & ——— Shaw	1860–61	yellow ware
Omaha	Omaha Pottery Co.	*c*.1884	stoneware
	Western Pottery Co.	*c*.1886–89	stoneware
Steele City	M. Randall	1886–87	?
	Joseph Porter	1890–91	?

NEW HAMPSHIRE

Boscaween	Jeremiah Burpee	1804–62	redware
Canaan	Isaac Lowell & Family	1818–72	redware

LOCALITY	POTTERY	PERIOD ACTIVE	TYPE OF WARE
Concord	Daniel Clark (Millville Pottery)	1791–1885	redware
	Richard Flanders	1813–24	redware
	Joseph Hazeltine	c.1845–80	redware
Exeter	Jabez Dodge & Sons (Exeter Pottery)	c.1771–1895	redware
Gonic	Elija Osborn & Sons	1839–85	redware
Keene	Hampshire Pottery	1871–c.90	redware
	Starkey & Howard	1871–74	redware, stoneware
Lyndeboro	Peter Clark & Sons	1775–1855	redware
Nashua	Martin Crafts	1838–52	stoneware
North Conway	Jethro Furber	1839–56	redware
Pottersville (Chesham)	Jedediah Southwick	1809–c.50	redware
	John D. Wright & Son	1845–c.60	redware
	Eben Russell & Sons	c.1850–60	redware
Troy	Solomon Goddard	c.1816–43	redware
West Plymouth	Peter Flanders	c.1840–56	redware
	William & John Gill	c.1830–86	redware

NEW JERSEY

LOCALITY	POTTERY	PERIOD ACTIVE	TYPE OF WARE
Bridgeton	George Hamlyn & Son (East Lake Pottery)	1835–c.1900	redware
Burlington	Daniel Coxe	c.1685–91	whiteware
Camden	Moro Phillips	1867–97	stoneware
Elizabeth	John M. Pruden & Co.	1816–79	stoneware, earthenware
	Andrew Forsyth	c.1865–67	redware
	L. S. Beerbauer	1879–1900	whiteware
Flemington	Fulper Pottery (Stangl Pottery)	1805–	stoneware, whiteware, redware

Appendix

LOCALITY	POTTERY	PERIOD ACTIVE	TYPE OF WARE
Gloucester	American Porcelain Man'f. Co.	1854–57	porcelain
	Gloucester Porcelain Co.	1857–c.72	porcelain
Jersey City	Jersey City Porcelain & Earthenware Co.	1825–28	porcelain
	D. & J. Henderson	1823–33	Rockingham, yellow ware
	American Pottery Manufacturing Co.	1833–57	Rockingham, yellow ware
	Jersey City Pottery Co.	1857–c.92	earthenware
Middletown	Van Schoik & Dun	c.1850–60	stoneware
Newark	B. J. Krumeich	c.1845–60	stoneware
	Philip Krumeich	1860–c.64	stoneware
	John Osborn (Newark Pottery)	c.1860–67	stoneware, earthenware
New Brunswick	A. J. Butler & Co.	c.1850–67	stoneware
	Horner & Shively	c.1831–41	stoneware
Perth Amboy	J. R. Watson	c.1833–40	stoneware
	A. Hall & Sons	c.1866	Rockingham, yellow ware
Rahway	Silas P. Leonard & Sons	c.1860–69	?
	William Turner	c.1868–70	Rockingham, yellow ware
	John Mann	c.1830–1900	redware
South Amboy	Warne & Letts	c.1778–1820	stoneware
	Humiston & Walker	c.1826–35	stoneware
	John Hancock	1829–40	Rockingham, yellow ware
	Swan Hill Pottery	1849–54	Rockingham, yellow ware

LOCALITY	POTTERY	PERIOD ACTIVE	TYPE OF WARE
	A. Cadmus (Congress Pottery)	c.1850	Rockingham, yellow ware
	Charles Coxon	c.1860	whiteware
	William Allen & Co.	c.1855–60	?
Trenton	Taylor & Co. (Trenton Pottery)	1852–72	Rockingham, yellow ware, whiteware
	Thomas Maddock & Co.	1875–1900	whiteware
	Rhodes & Co. (City Pottery)	1858–1900	whiteware
	William Young & Co.	1853–79	Rockingham, yellow ware, porcelain
	Willetts Manufacturing Company	1879–1900	porcelain, whiteware
	Burgess & Campbell (International Pottery Co.)	1879–1900	porcelain, whiteware
	Trenton China Co.	1859–91	porcelain
	Henry Speeler & Sons (Assanpink Pottery)	1864–c.79	porcelain, whiteware
	John Moses & Sons (Glasgow Pottery)	1860–90	Rockingham, yellow ware, whiteware
	Tams & Co. (Greenwood Pottery)	1861–c.1900	whiteware
	Charles Coxon & Co. (Empire Pottery)	1860–80	whiteware
	Ott & Co. (Eturia Works)	c.1863–92	Rockingham, whiteware porcelain

Appendix

LOCALITY	POTTERY	PERIOD ACTIVE	TYPE OF WARE
	Charles Cook	c.1870–1900	whiteware
	Mercer Pottery Co.	1869–1900	whiteware
	New Jersey Pottery Co.	1869–83	earthenware
	John S. & Howell McCully	c.1854–65	whiteware
	Eagle Pottery Co.	1882–95	whiteware
	Anchor Pottery	1894–1926	whiteware
	American Crockery Co.	1870–79	whiteware
	Union Pottery Co.	1869–89	whiteware
	Ira Cory & Co. (Mill Street Pottery)	c.1867–70	whiteware
	C. Moyer (National Pottery Co.)	c.1870	whiteware

NEW YORK

LOCALITY	POTTERY	PERIOD ACTIVE	TYPE OF WARE
Albany	Paul Cushman	c.1807–33	stoneware
	Moses Tyler	c.1826–47	stoneware
	Charles Dillon & Co.	1834–39	stoneware, earthenware
	Stephen Pepson	1866–90	stoneware
Athens	Nathan Clark & Co.	1805–38	stoneware, redware
	Ethan S. Fox	1838–43	stoneware
	Nathan Clark, Jr.	1843–91	stoneware
Baldwinsville	John Darrow & Sons	c.1845–76	stoneware
Bergholtz	Charles Mehwaldt	1851–85	redware
Binghamton	William Roberts (White's Pottery)	1848–88	stoneware
Buffalo	Charles W. Braun	1856–96	stoneware
	Henry Betz & Family	c.1857–1906	redware
Cortland	Thomas D. Chollar & Co.	1839–49	stoneware
	Madison Woodruff	1849–c.85	stoneware
Ellenville	Horace Weston & Sons	c.1829–70	stoneware
Elmira	James B. Farrington & Son	1867–c.95	stoneware

LOCALITY	POTTERY	PERIOD ACTIVE	TYPE OF WARE
Fort Edward	George Satterlee & Michael Morey	1861–85	stoneware
	Ottman Bros. & Co.	1872–c.92	stoneware
	Hilfinger Bros.	c.1888–1942	stoneware, redware
Fulton	Samuel Hart & Sons	1832–c.95	stoneware
Greenport	Austin Hempstead & Co.	c.1819–55	redware
	Thomas Hempstead	c.1850–72	stoneware, redware
Homer	Thomas D. Chollar & Co.	1832–44	stoneware
Huntington	Brown Brothers	1863–1904	stoneware, redware
Kings County (Brooklyn)	Thomas G. Boone & Sons	1839–46	stoneware
	Charles Cartlidge & Co.	c.1844–56	porcelain
	William Boch & Bros.	c.1844–62	porcelain
	Union Porcelain Works	c.1862–1908	porcelain
	James L. Jensen	c.1873–1915	porcelain
	Cornelius Vaupel	1878–94	stoneware, Rockingham
Lyons	Thompson Harrington	1852–72	stoneware
	Jacob Fisher & Co.	1872–1902	stoneware
Manhattan	Clarkson Crolius	c.1794–1838	stoneware
	Clarkson Crolius, Jr.	c.1835–49	stoneware, redware
	John Remmey, III	c.1791–1831	stoneware
	Thomas H. Commereau	1802–c.19	stoneware
	Washington Smith	1833–61	stoneware
	Lewis Lehman	1838–79	stoneware, redware
	James Carr & Co.	1856–88	Rockingham, porcelain, whiteware
	William Quenzer & Family	1850–83	redware

Appendix

LOCALITY	POTTERY	PERIOD ACTIVE	TYPE OF WARE
Morganville	Charles Ford	c.1870–1900	redware
Newburgh	Selah Reeve & Nathaniel Burling	c.1803–24	redware
Ogdensburg	Charles Hart	1850–58	stoneware
	William Hart	1858–69	stoneware
Oleon	Isaac H. Wands	1852–70	stoneware
Penn Yan	James Mantell	c.1855–76	stoneware
Poughkeepsie	Jacob Caire	c.1845–54	stoneware
	John B. Caire & Co.	1842–52	stoneware
	Adam Caire & Co.	1857–96	stoneware
Queens	William Boch, Jr.	c.1868–75	porcelain
	Louis E. Maidhoff	1879–c.82	porcelain
Rochester	John Burger & Son	1841–90	stoneware
	Frederick Stetzenmeyer & Co.	1849–60	stoneware
Rome	Norman L. Judd	1811–c.53	redware, stoneware
Sherburne	James Hart & Son	1841–85	stoneware
Syracuse	William H. Farrar	c.1841–72	stoneware, redware
	Onondaga Pottery Co. (Syracuse China Corp.)	1871–	whiteware, porcelain
	Charles E. Hubbell & Denison Chesebro	c.1867–87	stoneware
Troy	Israel Seymour & Co.	c.1819–52	stoneware, redware
	Walter J. Seymour	1852–58, 1861–85	stoneware
Utica	Noah White & Sons (Central New York Pottery)	1838–1909	stoneware
Watervaliet	William E. Warner	1829–52	Rockingham, whiteware stoneware
	Sanford S. Perry	1831–45	stoneware
	Porter & Fraser	1845–63	stoneware

LOCALITY	POTTERY	PERIOD ACTIVE	TYPE OF WARE

NORTH CAROLINA

LOCALITY	POTTERY	PERIOD ACTIVE	TYPE OF WARE
Bethabara	Gottfried Aust	1755–71	stoneware, redware, whiteware
	Rudolph Christ	1786–89	stoneware, redware, whiteware
Hickory	Hilton Pottery	c.1890–1900	stoneware
Lincolnton	T. Rhodes	c.1865–1900	stoneware
Salem	Gottfried Aust	1771–88	stoneware, redware, whiteware
	Rudolph Christ	1774–86, 1789–1823	stoneware, redware, whiteware
Seagrove	Cole Pottery	1891–1900	stoneware
	Rufus Owen	c.1900–17	stoneware
	Pascal Morable	c.1900–15	stoneware
Steeds	Peter Craven & Family	1750–1917	stoneware, redware
	James Fox	c.1860	stoneware

OHIO

LOCALITY	POTTERY	PERIOD ACTIVE	TYPE OF WARE
Akron	E. H. Merrill & Co. (Akron Pottery)	1847–94	whiteware
	W. H. Rockwell & Co.	1860–90	?
	Johnson & Dewey	c.1860–75	?
	Beecher & Lantz	c.1863–83	?
	United States Stoneware Co.	1885–1900	stoneware
	Summit China Co.	1890–1900	whiteware
	Weeks, Cook & Weeks	1882–1900	whiteware
Atwater	Caleb & Joshua Atwater	c.1830–40	stoneware
	Solomon Purdy	c.1850	stoneware, redware
	I. M. Mead & Co.	c.1840–60	stoneware
Bladensburg	J. G. Green	c.1866	?

Appendix

LOCALITY	POTTERY	PERIOD ACTIVE	TYPE OF WARE
Chatfield Corners	Eben French	c.1837–45	?
Chillicothe	George L. Wolf & B. Howson	c.1866	stoneware
Cincinnati	Peter Lessel & Family	1848–c.79	redware
	William Bromley & Sons	1843–70	whiteware, yellow ware
	George Scott & Sons	c.1846–1900	Rockingham, yellow ware
	M. Tempest & Co.	c.1859–88	Rockingham, yellow ware
	George & Andrew Biehn	1857–1900	?
	Fred Dallas (Dallas Pottery Co.)	1865–c.1900	?
	John Oehsle (Findlay Street Pottery)	c.1866–87	?
	Henry Mappes (Vine Street Pottery)	1859–1900	?
	August Mueller	1865–1900	?
Cleveland	Constantine Koch	c.1857–68	redware
	A. D. Higgins	c.1837–50	stoneware
	Daniel Fisk & Co.	c.1835–37	stoneware
Columbus	Frederick Abbe (Columbus Pottery)	c.1848–66	?
	Amon Jenkins & Son	c.1840–68	stoneware, earthenware
Crooksville	Lazalier Burley & Co.	c.1846–90	whiteware
Cuyahoga Falls	Camp, Cook & Co.	1863–80	?
	J. R. Thomas & Thomas Harris	c.1857–1900	?
Dayton	George Bisch	c.1858–68	redware
Doylestown	S. Routson	c.1835–46	stoneware

LOCALITY	POTTERY	PERIOD ACTIVE	TYPE OF WARE
East Liverpool	James Bennett & Bros.	c.1838–42	Rockingham, yellow ware
	S. & W. Baggott	1853–c.95	whiteware
	William Brunt, Sr.	1847–c.56	yellow ware
	Henry Brunt & Son	c.1856–1926	whiteware, yellow ware
	Booth Bros.	1858–65	?
	William Bloor	1859–62	yellow ware
	Brunt, Bloor, Martin & Co. (Dresden Pottery)	1875–92	whiteware, yellow ware
	Thomas Croxall & Co.	1844–98	whiteware, Rockingham, yellow ware
	Cartwright & Co.	1864–1900	whiteware
	East Liverpool Potteries Co.	1890–1900	whiteware
	Foster & Garner	1857–73	whiteware, Rockingham, yellow ware
	John Goodwin	1844–53	yellow ware
	Goodwin, Fleutke & Co.	1857–79	whiteware, yellow ware
	John Goodwin & Co. (Goodwin Pottery)	1844–1900	whiteware, yellow ware
	Globe Pottery Co.	1888–1900	whiteware
	Benjamin Harker & Sons (Wedgwood Pottery)	1877–81	whiteware
	George Harker & Co.	1847–90	whiteware, yellow ware
	John Henderson	c.1847–57	yellow ware

Appendix

LOCALITY	POTTERY	PERIOD ACTIVE	TYPE OF WARE
	Harrison, Fleutke & Co.	1874–81	whiteware
	Samuel & Elias Jackson	1868–79	?
	James McDevitt & Co. (California Pottery)	1867–1900	yellow ware
	A. H. Marks & Co.	1865–70	?
	George Morley & Co.	1884–90	whiteware
	McNichol, Burton & Co.	1870–92	whiteware
	D. E. McNichol Pottery Co.	1892–1900	whiteware
	William McCullough	1865–95	whiteware
	Potters' Cooperative Co.	1892–1900	?
	Salt & Mear (Mansion Pottery)	1841–c.53	yellow ware
	Henry Speeler	c.1850–52	yellow ware
	Sebring Pottery Co.	1887–1900	whiteware
	Schenkle, Allen & Co.	1881–88	whiteware
	C. C. Thompson & Co.	c.1868–95	whiteware
	R. Thomas & Sons	1873–1900	whiteware
	Vodrey Bros.	1857–c.1930	whiteware, Rockingham, yellow ware
	Elija Webster	1859–64	yellow ware
	Wylie Bros.	c.1848–54	yellow ware
	Woodward, Blakely & Co.	1849–57	yellow ware
	John Wylie (Great Western Pottery)	1874–c.1905	?
	Webster, Burgess & Viney	1867–69	?
	Samuel Worcester	1872–75	?
	Wallace & Chetwind	c.1881–1900	whiteware
	Knowles, Taylor & Knowles	c.1852–1926	whiteware, Rockingham, yellow ware

LOCALITY	POTTERY	PERIOD ACTIVE	TYPE OF WARE
Franklin	Franklin Porcelain Co.	c.1880–84	porcelain
Fultonham	Samuel Weller	1873–1900	whiteware, yellow ware
Massillon	Massillon Stoneware Co.	1882–1900	stoneware
Mogadore	J. H. Fenton	c.1854–75	stoneware
	Merrill, Earl & Ford	c.1880–1900	stoneware
Navarre	Navarre Stoneware Co.	c.1880–1900	stoneware
New Philadelphia	Nelson Tracy & Son	c.1865–90	?
Putnam	Solomon Purdy	c.1820	stoneware, redware
Roseville	Roseville Pottery Co.	c.1892–	whiteware, yellow ware
Salem	Salem China Co.	c.1896–	whiteware
Salineville	Carrollton China Co.	c.1901–10	whiteware
Steubenville	Steubenville Pottery Co.	1879–c.1900	whiteware
Wellsville	George Morley & Co. (Pioneer Pottery)	1878–1902	?
	Wellsville China Co.	c.1902–10	whiteware
	United States Pottery Co.	1898–1903	whiteware
Zanesville	Zanesville Stoneware Co.	1887–	stoneware

OREGON

LOCALITY	POTTERY	PERIOD ACTIVE	TYPE OF WARE
Albany	Barnet Ramsey & William Pollock	c.1862–64	stoneware
Buena Vista	William Ramsey, Jr., & —— Miller	c.1870–75	?
	Freeman Smith & Sons	1865–90	stoneware
Eola	S. H. Way	c.1863–68	redware
	William Ramsey, Jr.	1869–70	redware

Appendix

LOCALITY	POTTERY	PERIOD ACTIVE	TYPE OF WARE
Halsey	Barnet Ramsey	1864–68	stoneware
Portland	Oregon Pottery Co.	1885–96	stoneware
	Pacific Pottery Co.	1892–c.1950	stoneware
Springfield	Barnet Ramsey	c.1853–62	stoneware

PENNSYLVANIA

LOCALITY	POTTERY	PERIOD ACTIVE	TYPE OF WARE
Charlestown	Daniel High & Co. (Charlestown Pottery)	c.1817–31	redware
Downington	Thomas Vickers & Son	c.1796–1823	redware, whiteware
Greensburg	Michael Straw	c.1837	?
Harrisburg	Cowden & Wilcox (Harrisburg Stoneware Co.	c.1850–80	stoneware
Honey Brook	William Schofield	1891–1927	redware
Kennett Square	Edward Brosius	1841–85	redware
Lancaster	Conrad Gast	c.1843–68	redware
	Charles Schaeffer	c.1840	redware
Meyerstown	Henry McQuate	c.1845–59	?
New Castle	William Hill & Co.	1862–82	stoneware
	Chenango China Co.	c.1901–10	whiteware
Philadelphia	J. E. Jeffers & Co.	c.1868–1901	Rockingham, yellow ware
	Thomas Haig & Sons	c.1812–1900	Rockingham, yellow ware
	Abraham Miller	c.1840–58	Rockingham, whiteware, yellow ware
	Henry Remmey & Family	1810–	stoneware, porcelain
	Smith, Fife & Co.	c.1830	porcelain
	Isaac Spiegel, Jr.	c.1837–60	Rockingham, yellow ware

LOCALITY	POTTERY	PERIOD ACTIVE	TYPE OF WARE
	William Tucker & successors	1826–38	porcelain
	Alexander Trotter	c.1808–13	whiteware
Phoenixville	Phoenixville Pottery Co.	c.1867–92	Rocking-ham, white-ware, yel-low ware
	Chester Pottery Co.	c.1894–1903	whiteware
Pittsburgh	Alex Trotter & Co.	c.1815	whiteware
	Adam Burchfield	c.1860–65	stoneware, redware
	S. M. Kier & Co.	c.1863–70	earthenware
Waynesboro	John Bell	1833–80	stoneware, redware
	John W. Bell	1880–95	stoneware, redware
	Upton Bell	1895–99	stoneware, redware
Wellsville	Samuel Wells	c.1830	stoneware
Williamsport	W. A. Sloatman & J. Ream	c.1860–70	stoneware

RHODE ISLAND

East Greenwich	Samuel & Isaac Upton	c.1771–78	redware
Pawtucket	Joseph Wilson	c.1767–70	redware
Providence	Joseph Wilson	c.1770–80	redware

SOUTH CAROLINA

Bath	Thomas J. Davies	c.1861–65	stoneware
Bethune	Bethune Pottery	c.1870–	stoneware
Camden	Richard Champion	c.1784–91	redware (?)
Charlestown	John Bartlam	c.1770–72	whiteware
Kaolin	William H. Farrar (Southern Porce-lain Manufactur-ing Co.)	1856–78	whiteware, porcelain
New Windsor	Andrew Duché	c.1735	redware

187

Appendix

LOCALITY	POTTERY	PERIOD ACTIVE	TYPE OF WARE

TENNESSEE

LOCALITY	POTTERY	PERIOD ACTIVE	TYPE OF WARE
Baxter	Lafever Pottery	*c.*1840–1900	stoneware
	William Hedicaugh	*c.*1870–1900	stoneware
	Monroe Vickers	*c.*1880–1900	stoneware
Blountsville	William Wolfe	*c.*1848–78	redware
Chattanooga	Montague Pottery	*c.*1875–1900	stoneware
Daisey	C. L. Krager	*c.*1870–1900	stoneware
Happy Valley	William Grindstaff	*c.*1865–88	redware
	J. D. Garner	1888–96	?
Nashville	Harley Pottery	*c.*1875–1900	stoneware
Paris	Russell Pottery	*c.*1855–1900	stoneware
Sulphur Fork	Adam Cable	*c.*1869–75	stoneware

TEXAS

LOCALITY	POTTERY	PERIOD ACTIVE	TYPE OF WARE
Atacosa	William Meyer & Sons	*c.*1887–1940	stoneware, redware
Athens	Miller Pottery	*c.*1890–1910	stoneware
Cornersville	Schlender Pottery	*c.*1905–08	stoneware
Debny	Denny Pottery	*c.*1908	stoneware
Denton	J. Sublitz	*c.*1900–10	stoneware
	D. B. Dougherty	*c.*1900–08	stoneware
	A. H. Moss	*c.*1905	stoneware
Elmendorf	Saenger's Pottery	*c.*1880–1910	stoneware
	Star Pottery	1888–1914	stoneware
	E. Richter	*c.*1905–10	stoneware
Guadalupe County	Hirum Wilson	*c.*1870–84	stoneware
Henderson	J. F. Hunt	*c.*1898–1910	stoneware
	T. L. Hunt	*c.*1910	stoneware
	Russell Pottery	1900–*c.*09	stoneware
Lavernia	Littel's Pottery	*c.*1905–08	stoneware
Lloyd	M. B. Griffith	*c.*1908	stoneware
Marlin	Baker Pottery	*c.*1893	stoneware
Strumberg	J. F. W. Myers	*c.*1900–10	stoneware
Tyler	Liebrich Pottery Co.	*c.*1910	stoneware
Weatherford	R. Melcher	*c.*1907–08	stoneware, redware
Winnsboro	Winnsboro Pottery	*c.*1900–15	stoneware

188

LOCALITY	POTTERY	PERIOD ACTIVE	TYPE OF WARE

UTAH

LOCALITY	POTTERY	PERIOD ACTIVE	TYPE OF WARE
Brigham City	Fredrick F. Hansen	c.1855–85	redware
Fillmore	Ralph N. Rowley	c.1870	redware
Hyrum	James J. Hansen	c.1856–1909	redware
Provo	Peter Roberts	c.1865	redware
	A. H. Bowen	c.1871–75	redware
	E. C. Henrichsen & Co.	1874–c.1925	redware
	William D. Roberts (Zion Cooperative Pottery)	c.1870	redware
Salt Lake City	Bedsen & James Eardley	c.1875	redware
	Frederick Petersen	c.1852–70	redware
	William & Benjamin Blake	c.1875	redware
St. George	John Eardley	c.1853–80	redware
Vernal	Ephraim Roberts	c.1870–80	redware

VERMONT

LOCALITY	POTTERY	PERIOD ACTIVE	TYPE OF WARE
Bennington	Luman Norton & Co.	1823–28	stoneware, redware
	Luman Norton	1828–33	stoneware, redware
	Luman Norton & Son	1833–38	stoneware, redware
	Julius Norton	1838–45	stoneware, redware
	Norton & Fenton	1845–47	stoneware, redware
	Julius Norton	1847–50	stoneware, redware
	Julius & Edward Norton	1850–59	stoneware, redware
	Julius Norton & Co.	1859–61	stoneware, redware
	L. P. & Edward Norton	1861–81	stoneware, redware
	Edward Norton	1881–83	stoneware, redware

Appendix

LOCALITY	POTTERY	PERIOD ACTIVE	TYPE OF WARE
	Edward Norton & Co.	1883–94	stoneware, redware
	Jonathan Fenton	1847–48	Rockingham, yellow ware
	Lyman, Fenton & Park	1848	Rockingham, whiteware, yellow ware
	U.S. Pottery Co. (Lyman Fenton & Co.)	1849–58	whiteware, porcelain, Rockingham, yellow ware
Burlington	Nichols & Co.	1854–60	stoneware, Rockingham
	A. K. Ballard & Co.	c.1856–72	stoneware, Rockingham
	F. Woodworth	1872–c.85	stoneware
East Dorset	Jonathan Fenton & Sons	1810–c.35	stoneware, redware
Fairfax	George W. Farrar & J. H. Farrar	c.1840–59	stoneware
	Lewis & Cady	c.1858–59	stoneware
Middlebury	Caleb Farrar	1812–50	redware
New Haven	Caleb Wright	c.1830–40	redware
St. Johnsbury	William Hutchinson	c.1815–40	redware
	Richard Fenton & Co.	1808–59	stoneware
West Woodstock	Moses Bradley	1800–24	redware

VIRGINIA

LOCALITY	POTTERY	PERIOD ACTIVE	TYPE OF WARE
Alexandria	John Swann	c.1840	stoneware
	Benedict C. Milburn & Sons	c.1841–67	stoneware

190

LOCALITY	POTTERY	PERIOD ACTIVE	TYPE OF WARE
Big Spring Gap	William Wolfe	1875–81	stoneware
Chambersburg	John Bell	c.1827–33	redware
Petersburg	John Ducey	c.1866–69	?
Richmond	David Parr & Sons	c.1866–70	stoneware
Strassburg	Samuel Bell	1833–53	stoneware, redware
	Samuel & Solomon Bell	1853–82	stoneware, redware
	Samuel Bell & Sons	1882–1908	stoneware, redware
	Samuel H. Sonner	1853–62, 1870–92	redware
	J. M. Hickerson	c.1884–98	redware
	Amos Keister & Co.	1850–70	redware
	Jacob Eberley (Star Pottery)	1880–1900	redware
	William H. Lehew & Co.	c.1880–1900	redware
	L. D. Funkhouser	1889–1905	redware
	George W. Miller	c.1896–1900	redware
Wilson's Landing	Moro Philips	c.1850–58	stoneware
Winchester	Peter Bell	1824–45	redware
	Anthony W. Baecher	1870–89	redware

WASHINGTON

Spokane	William Ramsey, Jr.	c.1875	?

WEST VIRGINIA

Chester	Taylor, Smith & Taylor	c.1890–1945	whiteware
Columbus	Schenk & Rocker	c.1870–1900	stoneware
East River	Brown & McKenzie	c.1870–1900	stoneware
Freeman's Landing	Carlyle & McFadden	c.1850–55	stoneware
Martinsburg	James Weise	c.1870	?

Appendix

LOCALITY	POTTERY	PERIOD ACTIVE	TYPE OF WARE
Morgantown	John W. Thompson & Son	c.1800–90	stoneware
	——— Faulke	c.1785	redware
Newell	Edwin M. Knowles China Co.	1854–c.1950	whiteware
New Cumberland	Chelsea China Co.	c.1888–1904	whiteware, earthenware
Parkersburg	Donahue Pottery	1866–1908	stoneware
Wellsburg	H. N. Bakewell	c.1831–41	stoneware
West Liberty	David Shorts	c.1850–55	?
Wheeling	Wheeling Pottery Co.	c.1877–1904	whiteware
	Ohio Valley China Co.	c.1890–1900	whiteware, porcelain
	Warwick China Co.	1877–c.1904	whiteware
	Wheeling Potteries Co.	c.1903–05	

WISCONSIN

LOCALITY	POTTERY	PERIOD ACTIVE	TYPE OF WARE
Belmont	John Hammett & Bro.	c.1842–79	redware
Broadhead	William Murrey	c.1868	redware
Franklin	Konrad Langenberg	c.1860–88	redware
Manitowac	William Reinhardt	c.1868–69	?
Menasha	Batchelder Pottery	c.1850–80	?
Milwaukee	Isaac P. Brazelton	c.1844–55	stoneware
	Charles Hermann & Co.	1856–1902	stoneware
	Frederick & Albert Hermann	1857–98	redware
	John G. Bauer	1857–1905	redware
	Frank Mohr	1856–66	redware
	Wentzel Weitzner	1856–96	redware
	Caspar Hennecke & Co.	1868–95	stoneware
	John G. Heinze	1867–94	redware
	H. Weis & F. Schmidt	1876–1915	?

LOCALITY	POTTERY	PERIOD ACTIVE	TYPE OF WARE
Sheboygan	Theodore Gunther (Eastern Stoneware Factory)	*c.*1862–87	stoneware
	Mies Diedrich & Co.	*c.*1887–90	stoneware
Whitewater	Warren Cole & Co.	*c.*1845–55	redware
	J. C. Williams & Co.	1855–59	redware
	Cole & Hunter	1859–67	redware
	Daniel Cole	1867–71	redware
	Michael Ohnhaus & Co.	1859–*c.*65, 1871–81	redware

Index

INDEX

Provo, Utah, redware potteries, 43
Pruden & Olcott, 57
Purdy, Solomon, 33

Queensware, 121

Rahway, New Jersey
  redware pottery, 23
  yellow ware, 99
Ramsey, Barnet, 89
Red Wing, Minnesota
  redware potteries, 36–37
  stoneware, 81
  yellow ware, 112
Red Wing Stoneware Company, Red Wing, Minnesota, 81, 112
Redware, techniques of manufacture, 3–13
Remmey, Joseph H., 57
Remmey Pottery, Philadelphia, Pennsylvania, 58–59, 149
Richmond, Indiana, brown & yellow ware pottery, 111
Richmond, Virginia, stoneware pottery, 68
Rieta ware, 130
Ripley, Illinois
  stoneware pottery, 78
  yellow ware, 111–112
Rockingham glaze, 95–96, 99–100
Roof tile, 33–34
Roseville Pottery Company, Roseville, Ohio, 109
Routson, S., 76
Runey, John, 15
Russell Pottery, Henderson, Texas, 88

Sackett, Alfred M., 35
Sacramento Pottery, Sacramento, California, 89
Saenger, William, 87
Saggers, defined, 146
St. Charles, Missouri, redware potteries, 38
St. Johnsbury, Vermont, stoneware pottery, 62–63
Saint Nicholas pitcher, 131

Salamander Works, Woodbridge, New Jersey, 98
Salem China Company, Salem, Ohio, 138
Salem, North Carolina
  redware pottery, 28–29
  stoneware, 70
  whiteware, 133–134
Salt glaze, 50
Salt Lake City, Utah, redware potteries, 44
Savannah, Georgia, porcelain manufactory, 154
Scott, George C. & sons, 76, 110
Seymour, Nathenial & family, 17, 64
Sgraffito decoration, 10–11
Sheboygan, Wisconsin, stoneware potteries, 82
Shenango Pottery Company, New Castle, Pennsylvania, 130
Shepardstown, West Virginia, redware potteries, 30
Slip cup, defined, 10
Smith, Cass, 79
Smith, Fife & Company, 149
Smith, Freeman & sons, 90, 102
Soft paste porcelain, 146
Sohns, George M., 39
Somerset, Massachusetts
  redware potteries, 15–16
  stoneware, 63
  brown & yellow ware, 102
Sonner, Samuel H. & sons, 68
South Amboy, New Jersey
  stoneware potteries, 56–57
  brown & yellow ware, 97, 98–99
South Carolina
  stoneware potteries, 71
  whiteware, 132
  porcelain, 154
Southern Porcelain Manufacturing Company, Kaolin, South Carolina
  whiteware, 132–133
  porcelain, 154
Spongeware, 142
Spring Garden Pottery, Philadelphia, Pennsylvania, 101–102

202